BOOK*KEEPING*

FOR BUSINESS OWNERS

What Readers Are Saying . . .

Bookkeeping for Business Owners: Gaining Clarity and Confidence without the Overwhelm is a game-changer for anyone struggling with business finances. The author breaks down bookkeeping in a simple, relatable, and empowering way that makes the process feel doable—even for non-numbers people! This book is not just informative, it's inspiring. Every entrepreneur, especially women in business, needs this guide on their shelf.

— Valorie Bennett-Wiley, Pastor Emerita and Financial Officer

As someone who has studied business finance extensively in undergraduate school and as a small business owner, I know how stressful keeping up with your books can be. Valaise breaks it all the way down in a way that feels doable and clear, without the overwhelm. She has a gift for making it simple, practical, and empowering. This is the kind of guidance every entrepreneur needs to keep their business on track.

— Chanel Oldham, Howard University Alum/Business Owner

Bookkeeping for Business Owners: Gaining Clarity and Confidence without the Overwhelm is a smart, structured, and encouraging resource for anyone navigating opening a new business and how to manage your journey. Valaise offers real-life insights on building partnerships, responding to feedback, and tightening your bookkeeping with clarity and professionalism. The tone is conversational yet informative, making it approachable and easy to read. The action items at the end of each section give it a hands-on, workshop feel, helping readers turn advice into concrete next steps.

— Denise Everett, Retired Business owner with 30 years of HR experience

BOOKKEEPING FOR BUSINESS OWNERS

Gaining clarity and confidence without the overwhelm

Valaise Smith, EA

WRITEWAY PUBLISHING
Raleigh, North Carolina
www.writewaypublishing.com

Bookkeeping for Business Owners

Disclaimer: This book was written for general educational and informational purposes only. Nothing in this book should be construed as professional accounting, tax, or financial advice or applicable for any reader's particular needs. The content is presented "as is" for illustrative and general purposes. Neither the author nor the publisher make any guarantees or promises regarding reader outcome and disclaim any and all liability for any loss or disruption of any sort that may be incurred as a result of relying on information contained in this book. While this book is a valuable resource, it is incumbent on the reader to seek individual professional guidance for their own specific financial, tax, and legal financial needs. Tax laws change over time, and software products update and change as well. References to such in this book are current at the time of publishing.

Note: All examples, charts, and illustrations in this book are original educational content created solely for instructional purposes. They are not actual company financials and are not affiliated with, endorsed by, or sourced from any accounting software provider (such as QuickBooks, Xero, or Wave). Any resemblance to specific reports or formats is purely for illustrative purposes.

ISBN 978-1-956543-87-2
Printed in the United States of America

Book layout by CSinclaire Write-Design LLC
Cover by Travis J. Norman, Norman Collective Group, LLC

WRITEWAY PUBLISHING
Raleigh, North Carolina
www.writewaypublishing.com

CONTENTS

FOREWORD

Every so often you encounter someone who has the rare gift of turning confusion into clarity. Valaise Smith is one of those people. With over 25 years of real experience as a financial professional, trust and believe that Valaise KNOWS her stuff!

I've had the privilege of working with Valaise over an extended period of time—first as a student in my four-day speaker training called Crush The Stage, then for an entire year under my direct tutelage, and eventually as a trusted professional inside my own business. Throughout that journey, what stood out most was not just her technical expertise, but her deep understanding of the entrepreneurial mind. She knows that most business owners aren't afraid of hard work—they're overwhelmed by uncertainty.

Bookkeeping for Business Owners—Gaining Clarity and Confidence without the Overwhelm was written for that exact entrepreneur, and I can't wait for your business to benefit from Valaise's decades of experience and expertise like I have.

Too many business owners build incredible visions while quietly feeling disconnected from their numbers. They're generating revenue but are unsure how money is flowing, where it's being wasted, or how to use financial information to make confident decisions. Valaise meets that overwhelm with structure, simplicity, and compassion. Her Tried and True frameworks don't just explain bookkeeping—they create clarity.

What makes this work especially powerful is that it's practical and proven.

I trusted Valaise enough to hire her inside my own company to handle accounting and bookkeeping, and I personally implemented the same principles you'll find in these pages. The result was greater financial confidence, cleaner systems, and better decision-making. That's why I don't simply recommend this book—I stand behind it.

This book is also the result of obedience to a nudge. I had the honor of planting the seed that encouraged Valaise to write it, and watching her bring this message to life has been incredibly rewarding. She leads with integrity, patience, and a genuine desire to see entrepreneurs win.

If you are a serious business owner who wants to move from overwhelm to clarity and build a financially sound business with intention, this book will serve you well. Read it carefully. Apply it consistently. Your numbers can work for you—and Valaise will show you how.

— **Dr. Delatorro McNeal, II**
The TODAY Show Contributor, Peak Performance Expert,
Hall of Fame Keynote Speaker & WSJ / USA Today Bestselling Author
Shift Into a Higher Gear: Better Your Best and Live Life to the Fullest

My Why

As a financial professional, I wrote this book because I've witnessed too many passionate, talented entrepreneurs watch their dreams collapse due to preventable financial missteps. Small businesses truly are the heartbeat of the American economy, representing 99% of all businesses. Yet nearly half fail within their first five years, often due to poor cash flow management or lack of funding.

What breaks my heart is that it isn't usually because their business concept was flawed or their service wasn't needed. It's because they lacked the financial literacy skills and discipline to sustain the business. Many entrepreneurs can't access crucial funding simply because they haven't organized their finances in a way that demonstrates their true potential to lenders and investors.

I also wrote this book because I understand, personally, what it means to face unexpected challenges as a business owner and how crucial financial stability becomes during those times. In the beginning of my fifth year in business, I was diagnosed with breast cancer. Right in the middle of tax season, the busiest time of year for any tax professional.

What could have been a devastating blow to my business became a testament to the power of having strong financial foundations. Because I had implemented the very systems I teach in this book, my business was organized, my cash flow was predictable, and my clients trusted the financial processes we had in place. With the incredible support of my faith, family, friends, who were absolute rock stars, and clients who showed extraordinary understanding and support, I was able to persevere through one of the most challenging periods of my life without my business suffering.

That experience reinforced everything I believe about financial empowerment. When your books are straight and your financial systems are solid, you're not just prepared for growth, you're prepared for life's unexpected challenges. You have options, stability, and the peace of mind that comes from knowing your business can weather any storm.

I wrote this book to bridge that gap in financial literacy. I believe financial empowerment isn't just about numbers, it's about giving hardworking business owners the tools to protect their dreams. When a small business owner understands their financial story and can confidently manage their books, they gain more than organized records. They gain clarity and confidence without the overwhelm.

My mission is to transform bookkeeping from an intimidating obligation into an accessible tool for business growth. I want to demystify financial management with straightforward language and practical steps that even the most "numbers-averse" entrepreneur can implement. Because when small business owners master their finances, they don't just survive, they thrive, create jobs, strengthen communities, and build legacies!

This isn't just about balancing books. It's about balancing lives and creating opportunities for the backbone of our economy to stand strong!

1

Accounting Terms Made Simple

• Breaking down the secret language of business finance •

What Is Accounting and Why Does It Matter?

Let's start with the basics. Accounting is simply the process of recording your business financial transactions. Think of it as tracking money as it flows in and out of your business, who it flows from or to, and the amount of each transaction. That's it—*nothing to be afraid of!*

Understanding Your Business Financial Health

You've invested everything into your business: your time, your money, maybe even other people's money. Without proper accounting, you'll never have a true, real-time understanding of your company's health and value. As the owner, it's your responsibility to steward your company's assets and liabilities, but you can't do that without the right financial reports.

Becoming a Better Candidate for Funding

Unless you're independently wealthy, there will come a time when you need an infusion of cash. Your business might grow rapidly and need a line of credit, or you might face an unexpected setback requiring capital to keep operations running smoothly. Having current and accurate accounting records makes getting money from banks, investors, or even friends and family much easier. Good financial records demonstrate that you respect their investment and will safeguard their trust.

Reaching Your Goals Faster

Whether you want to sell your business, create a retirement income stream, or give back to your community, proper accounting provides the insights you need to make better financial decisions. Better decisions directly impact both the short-term and long-term success of your business. If you're making financial decisions by checking your bank balance and responding to whomever is calling for money, you're not managing your business—*your business is managing you.* Proper accounting best practices help you reach your goals faster by creating a clear roadmap to follow.

Long-Term Efficiency

The longer you wait to implement proper accounting, the more it will cost when you do. Starting from day one prevents costly mistakes that will eventually need correction. Manually sorting through hundreds or thousands of invoices and receipts months or years later costs exponentially more than implementing a simple system from the start.

Essential Accounting Terms Every Business Owner Should Know

Like any field, accounting has its own language. It's not about learning "jargon." You need to know the language and terminology used in practice in real life to make financial decisions and understand financial transactions.

Accounting

In every business, money comes in and money goes out. Accounting is simply tracking the who, where, when, why, and how of money flowing through your business, then reporting it.

Assets & Liabilities

Assets are anything your business owns: cash in the bank, accounts receivable, inventory, equipment, any tangible thing your company holds. The cost of an asset is not deducted on your P&L (profit & loss income statement).

Liabilities are what you owe to someone else: accounts payable, equipment loans, tax liabilities. Unless liabilities serve a specific strategic purpose, keep them to a minimum. Paying off a liability is not deducted on your P&L.

➥ When you buy equipment or inventory, you're not losing money, you're simply converting one asset (cash) into another asset (equipment or inventory). Since you still own something of value, this exchange doesn't affect your profitability, which is why asset purchases appear on your Balance Sheet rather than reducing profit on your P&L statement. In reverse, when you take on a liability like a loan, it's not recorded as income because you're simply exchanging one obligation for cash. This is why the loan shows up on your Balance Sheet instead of inflating your profit on the P&L.

Cost of Goods Sold

Cost of goods sold (COGS) refers to the direct costs of producing the goods sold by a company. This amount includes the cost of the materials and labor directly used to create the goods. You should not include indirect expenses, such as costs to distribute and/or sell the item, in your COGS numbers.

Cost of goods sold is also referred to as "cost of sales."

Debits & Credits

Debits and credits represent entries in your General Ledger (the chronological list of every financial transaction or Cash Flow Statement). Credits appear on the right side, debits on the left. For every credit entry, there must be a balancing debit entry. Unless you're in the accounting business, that's all you need to know because the accounting system handles the heavy lifting behind the scenes.

Double Entry Accounting

Double-entry accounting shows both sides of any transaction. For example: You buy a $200 printer for your business. You debit your checking account for $200 and credit your expense account for $200. You took $200 from one account

Double-Entry Accounting Example

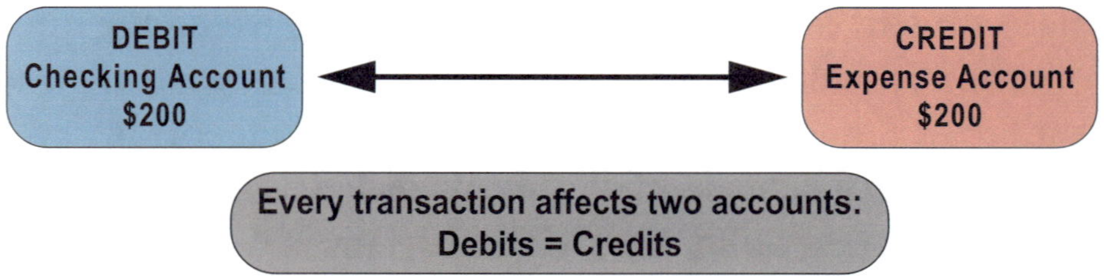

Example: You buy a $200 printer. Money leaves your Checking Account (Debit) and is recorded as an Expense (Credit). Balance is maintained.

and tracked where it went—pretty simple! This system maintains balance by displaying paired debits and credits for every financial move.

Profit & Loss Statement

Your Profit & Loss (P&L) Statement reports income and expenses from business operations for a set time period. It tracks money coming in and money going out. It's the bottom-line indicator of how your business performed during the chosen period. Your annual P&L, along with other reports, positions you to file a timely and accurate income tax return.

Expenses

Anything your business pays for that's deducted in the current period is an expense for that period. When expenses exceed income, you're losing money. Too many expenses exceeding income will force you out of business.

General Ledger

Your General Ledger is a recording of all your debits and credits. It's a record of your complete financial transaction history.

Balance Sheet

A Balance Sheet is a snapshot of your business financial position at any given point in time. It shows the balances of assets, liabilities, and equity accounts, reflecting your business net worth. It reveals how liquid your business is, how burdened with debt, and what equity you hold. Banks often analyze balance sheets to determine financing eligibility.

Fixed vs. Variable Costs

Fixed costs are regular expenses that don't fluctuate with sales: rent, internet, phone bills. These expenses are sometimes called "overhead" or "general & administrative" expenses.

Variable costs change based on production or sales volume. If you manufacture wooden sheds, wood costs vary based on how many sheds you produce. Marketing, commissions, shipping, and royalties can also be variable expenses.

Owner's Equity

As the business owner, you own the assets minus the liabilities of your business. What's left is your equity. This adjusts annually based on the profits or losses for that year and any distributions paid from the company to owners.

Cash vs. Accrual Accounting

There are two different reporting methods in accounting:

Cash method: Records income when you actually receive money and expenses when you actually spend it. Real-time reflection of your current financial position.

Accrual method: Records transactions when created. An invoice shows as sales even before payment is received, and expenses show when incurred even before bills are paid. This gives a pure reflection of business activity, though some invoices may become bad debts. For tax purposes, businesses with inventory typically report on accrual basis, while those without inventory use cash basis.

Key Takeaway

Accounting does not have to be mysterious or complicated. It's simply organized tracking of your money movements. Understanding these basic terms and concepts gives you the foundation to make informed financial decisions and build a successful business. The language of accounting becomes your roadmap to financial clarity and business growth without the overwhelm.

> **Remember**: *You don't need to become an accountant, but understanding these fundamentals puts you in control of your business finances rather than letting them control you.*

In addition to breaking down the secret language of business finances, I've created a **Financial Toolkit** as a free gift to support you beyond these pages. Think of it as a ready-made starting point—a set of practical tools and checklists that guide you through the essentials of managing your finances. Instead of staring at a blank page and wondering where to begin, this toolkit gives you a clear framework you can put into action right away. It's designed to help you organize, plan, and take the next step toward financial confidence with ease.

Grab your free tool kit: www.triedandtruefs.com/financialtoolkit

2

Connecting Your Financial Accounts

• Bringing your money into focus •

Making the Connection: Your Financial Lifeline

One of the first things you will do after purchasing your accounting system is to connect your business financial accounts to it. This is where your accounting transforms from a manual chore into an automated powerhouse that saves you hours every month.

Think of account connections as creating a direct pipeline between your banking activity and your accounting records. Instead of manually entering every transaction, your accounting software will automatically download and categorize most of your financial activity, leaving you with the task to simply review (carefully and thoughtfully) and approve.

Which Accounts Should You Connect?

Essential Business Accounts

Connect all accounts that are exclusively used for business purposes. These might include:

- **Business Checking Account:** This is typically your primary operating account where customer payments are deposited and business expenses are paid.
- **Business Savings Account:** Whether you use this for emergency funds, tax savings, or retained earnings, connecting it ensures you track all interest earned and transfers.
- **Business Credit Cards:** These are powerful tools for expense tracking and cash flow management. Connecting them automatically categorizes your purchases and tracks outstanding balances.
- **Business Lines of Credit:** If you have access to business credit lines, connecting them helps you monitor usage and payments. This will show up on your balance sheet.
- **Business Investment Accounts:** Any business-owned investment accounts should be connected to track gains, losses, and dividend income. Now, I don't want to complicate this process or confuse you, but I have a simple tactical tip to share.

P.O.T.S.™ for Financial Clarity

One of the simplest ways to take control of your cash flow is by dividing your revenue into four "pots": Payroll, Operating expenses, Taxes, and Savings. Each pot is assigned a percentage of your revenue in advance—for example, 40% for payroll, 30% for operating expenses, 20% for taxes, and 10% for savings. This structure ensures that money is automatically set aside for the most important functions of your business, so you're never caught off guard when quarterly taxes are due or when it's time to pay yourself. By following P.O.T.S.™, you'll create smoother operations and reduce the overwhelm that comes with managing your finances.

The Personal Account Dilemma

Let's address the elephant in the room. Many business owners, especially in the early stages of the business, use personal accounts for business expenses. Maybe you used your personal credit card for office supplies or paid a vendor from your personal checking account.

This is a NO JUDGMENT ZONE. It happens to the best of us, and there's a way to handle it properly.

Manual Entry for Personal Accounts Used for Business

Please DO NOT connect personal accounts to your business accounting system. Instead, manually enter business expenses that were paid from personal accounts.

Here's how:

1. Create an "Owner Contribution" or "Owner's Equity" account in your chart of accounts

2. Record the business expense in the appropriate expense category

3. Record the payment source as coming from your owner contribution account

4. Keep detailed records of these transactions with receipts and documentation

For example, if you bought $200 in office supplies with your personal credit card:

- **Debit:** Office Supplies $200
- **Credit:** Owner Contribution $200

This properly reflects that you personally funded a business expense, which may be reimbursable to you later or treated as additional investment in the business.

Where the Comingling Train Stops

While we're not judging past comingling, this is where it stops. Moving forward, maintain strict separation between personal and business finances. This separation is crucial for:

- **Tax compliance:** Creating clear business expense documentation
- **Legal protection:** Maintaining corporate veil if you're incorporated
- **Financial clarity:** Understanding true business profitability without the overwhelm or confusion
- **Professional credibility:** Providing clean books for lenders and investors
- **Audit protection:** Offering clear paper trails

Make a CEO move and open dedicated business accounts, if you haven't already, and commit to using them exclusively for business purposes going forward.

One Business, One Set of Books

Please DO NOT connect accounts from multiple businesses to the same accounting file. This is a critical rule that prevents confusion and ensures accurate financial reporting.

Each business entity needs its own separate accounting system for multiple reasons:

- **Legal Requirements:** Different business entities have different tax obligations and reporting requirements. Mixing them creates compliance nightmares.

- **Financial Clarity:** You need to understand the individual profitability, cash flow, and financial position of each business. Combined records and comingled funds make this difficult or impossible.

- **Professional Standards:** Banks, investors, and potential buyers expect clean, separated financial records for each business entity.

- **Tax Complication Reduction:** Each business files its own tax return. Combined records make tax preparation exponentially more complex and expensive.

If you operate multiple businesses, set up separate accounting files for each entity, even if you use the same accounting software. Most modern platforms allow multiple company files under one user account.

Setting Your Historical Starting Point

When you connect accounts, the system may ask how far back you want to pull transaction history. This decision impacts your workload and the usefulness of your financial reports. Typically, most financial institutions will allow you to go back 90 days.

Recommended Starting Points

- **Most Recent Calendar or Fiscal Year:** Start with January 1 of your current tax year if you're on a calendar year or else the beginning of your current fiscal year. This provides a complete picture of your current year's performance without overwhelming you with historical data.

- **Beginning of Upcoming Tax Year:** If you're connecting accounts late in the year and have already filed taxes for previous periods, start with the upcoming tax year. There's no need to recreate work that's already been completed and filed.

Why Not Go Back Further?

While it might seem logical to import every available transaction, consider these factors:

- **Workload Management:** Each imported transaction needs review and categorization. Importing years of data can create an overwhelming backlog.

- **Historical Relevance:** Very old transactions may not reflect your current business operations and could skew trend analysis.

- **Tax Filing Status:** If you've already filed tax returns for previous years, recreating that data in your accounting system doesn't provide additional value unless you're conducting a specific analysis.

***Pro Tip: Security Considerations* —** Modern accounting software uses bank-level encryption and read-only access to your accounts. The software cannot initiate transactions or transfers—it can only read transaction data.

However, account security will be strengthened if you will do these things:

- Use strong, unique passwords for your accounting software

- Enable two-factor authentication when available

- Regularly review connected accounts for any unauthorized access
- Disconnect accounts immediately if you suspect any security breach

Post-Connection Setup

Daily Feeds

Most banks update transaction data daily, usually overnight. Your accounting software will automatically download new transactions, typically categorizing them based on previous patterns or merchant information. However, I strongly recommend that you review the data carefully to ensure your transactions are being categorized properly.

Review Routine

Establish a routine for reviewing and approving downloaded transactions. Many business owners find success with regular reviews.

- Weekly detailed reviews: 15 to 30 minutes for thorough categorization and posting transactions
- Monthly reconciliation: 30 to 60 minutes to reconcile (compare) your accounting records to bank statements

Troubleshooting Common Issues

Connection Errors: Banks occasionally update their systems, breaking the connection. Most accounting software provides easy reconnection tools. Look out for the warning message on your accounting dashboard.

Duplicate Transactions: If you manually entered transactions before connecting accounts, you may create duplicates. Most software has tools to identify and merge duplicates. However, as a best practice, always be sure to click the button to "update transactions" before you start manually entering missing transactions.

Missing Transactions: Occasionally, transactions may not download. Regular reconciliation helps identify and manually add any missing items while the information is fresh in your mind.

Categorization Errors: The software's automatic categorization isn't perfect. Regular review ensures transactions are properly classified.

The Foundation for Automated Bookkeeping

Properly connecting your financial accounts transforms your bookkeeping from a time-consuming manual process into an efficient, automated system. This foundation allows you to focus on analyzing your financial data rather than just recording it, leading to strategic business decisions and improved profitability.

The accounting software world changes fast. What's recommended today may not even exist tomorrow. That's why I've created the Tried and True **Resource Guide**, a living list of bookkeeping and accounting tools I keep updated with the latest options, features, and my personal recommendations.

Download your free copy at
www.triedandtruefs.com/resourceguide
and get instant access to these resources:

- My top picks for bookkeeping and accounting software (with pros and cons)
- Checklists to help you decide which tool fits your stage of business

- Exclusive bonus resources and updates you won't find in this book

Your tools should work as hard as you do and this Tried and True Resource Guide will help you stay up to date without the overwhelm.

At the end of the day, there's no one "perfect" accounting software. The key is to start with something that fits your business right now and that you'll actually use. Then you can grow into more advanced tools as your business expands. Remember, the software is just a tool. The real power comes from you showing up consistently and staying on top of your numbers. Once you've got that rhythm, you'll not only keep your books straight but also feel way more confident about every decision you make for your business.

> **REMEMBER:** *The goal isn't just to connect accounts, it's to create a reliable, efficient system that provides accurate, timely financial information to take your business to the next level.*

3

Setting Up Your Chart of Accounts

• Building the foundation for financial success •

The Backbone of Your Financial System

Think of your chart of accounts as the DNA of your financial system. It's basically a list of accounts that determines how every dollar flowing through your business gets categorized, tracked, and reported, because every dollar needs a destination.

Your chart of accounts is essentially a comprehensive list of all the accounts you'll use in the course of running your business. It's like creating labeled filing cabinets for your money. Some cabinets hold information about money coming in (income accounts), others track money going out (expense accounts), and still others keep track of what you own and owe (asset and liability accounts).

This isn't optional, your chart of accounts directly impacts every financial report you'll ever generate. It feeds information to your P&L, populates your Balance

Sheet, and forms the foundation for every business decision you'll make based on financial data.

Understanding the Structure

Income and Expense Accounts: Your P&L Foundation

Income and expense accounts form the operational heart of your business and flow directly to your P&L (also called an Income Statement). These accounts tell the story of your day-to-day business activities.

- **Income** accounts capture all the ways money flows into your business:
  - Product sales
  - Service revenue
  - Consulting fees
  - Interest earned
  - Rental income
  - Commission income

- **Expense** accounts track where your money goes to operate the business:
  - Cost of goods sold
  - Rent and utilities
  - Office supplies
  - Marketing and advertising
  - Professional services
  - Travel and entertainment
  - Insurance
  - Equipment purchases

Asset and Liability Accounts: Your Balance Sheet Structure

Asset and liability accounts, along with equity accounts, flow to your Balance Sheet and provide a snapshot of your business financial position at any given moment.

- **Asset** accounts represent what your business **owns:**
  - Cash and bank accounts
  - Accounts receivable (money customers owe you)
  - Inventory
  - Equipment and machinery
  - Vehicles
  - Prepaid expenses
  - Investments
- **Liability** accounts track what your business **owes:**
  - Accounts payable (money you owe vendors)
  - Credit card balances
  - Loans and mortgages
  - Accrued expenses
  - Payroll liabilities
  - Tax obligations
- **Equity** accounts show your **ownership** stake:
  - Owner's equity
  - Retained earnings
  - Owner draws or distributions

The Tax Form Strategy: Your Secret Weapon

Here's a pro tip that will make your accountant's day (and save you money at tax time):

> ***Pro Tip:*** Use your corresponding tax form for your business structure as your chart of accounts guide. This strategic approach ensures you have all the accounts listed on your tax form in your accounting system and will put you in the driver's seat when tax time comes without the overwhelm!

Tax Forms by Business Structure

Sole Proprietorship (Schedule C): Your chart of accounts should mirror the income and expense categories on Schedule C, including specific expense categories like advertising, car and truck expenses, insurance, legal and professional services, and office expenses.

Partnership (Form 1065): Structure your accounts to align with partnership tax reporting requirements, including separate tracking for guaranteed payments and partner distributions.

S Corporation (Form 1120-S): Include accounts for officer compensation, other deductions, and shareholder distributions to match S-Corp tax reporting needs.

C Corporation (Form 1120): Set up accounts that correspond to corporate tax categories, including specific deduction categories and retained earnings tracking.

This alignment strategy means that when tax season arrives, your bookkeeper or accountant can easily pull the information needed for each segment of your tax return. Instead of spending hours reorganizing and reclassifying transactions, the data flows naturally from your accounting system to your tax forms. Your accountant will absolutely love you for this foresight!

Starting with Your System's Default Setup

Most modern accounting systems (QuickBooks, Xero, FreshBooks, etc.) will automatically generate a standard chart of accounts based on the business type you select during setup. This is actually a helpful starting point because the software developers have done the heavy lifting of determining which accounts most businesses in your industry typically need. However, don't just accept the default setup and call it a day. These generic charts of accounts are built for the "average" business in your category, but your business isn't average, it's unique with its own specific needs, revenue streams, and expense patterns.

Customization: Making It Work for Your Business

Renaming Accounts for Clarity

The default account names your software suggests might not make immediate sense to you or your team. Don't hesitate to rename accounts to something more intuitive and recognizable for your specific business.

For example:

- Change "Other Income" to "Affiliate Commissions" if such commissions provide a significant revenue stream for you. The key is using terminology that you and your team will understand and use consistently.

Creating Strategic Sub-Accounts

Sub-accounts (or sub-categories) are where the real power of customization comes into play. They allow you to drill down into specific areas of your business to capture data that will allow for strategic decision-making.

- **Revenue Sub-Accounts Example:** Instead of just having "Services or Sales of Product Income," consider breaking it down:

REVENUE SUB ACCOUNT EXAMPLE			
PRODUCT INCOME	$	SERVICE INCOME	$
ONLINE COURSE	$	CONSULTING	$
BRANDED MERCHANDISE	$	BOOKKEEPING	$
TAX PREP	$		

This breakdown helps you understand which products or services are driving the most revenue in your business and where to focus your growth efforts.

- **Expense Sub-Account Example:** Rather than lumping everything into "Marketing Expenses," create sub-accounts like:

EXPENSE SUB ACCOUNT EXAMPLE	
MARKETING	$
DIGITAL ADVERTISING	$
WEBSITE	$
PROMOTIONAL ITEMS	$
CONTENT CREATION	$
SOCIAL MEDIA MANAGEMENT	$

This detailed tracking can reveal which marketing channels are providing the best return on investment in a given period, enabling you to allocate your marketing budget more effectively.

Geographic or Department Tracking

If your business operates in multiple locations or has distinct departments, consider incorporating this into your chart of accounts structure.

By location

- Revenue: East Coast
- Revenue: West Coast
- Rent: Detroit Office
- Rent: Phoenix Office

By department

- Payroll: Sales Team
- Payroll: Operations Team
- Travel: Business Development
- Travel: Conferences

Chart of Accounts

- 1000 — Assets
  - 1010 — Cash
  - 1020 — Accounts Receivable
  - 1030 — Prepaid Expenses
  - 1040 — Inventory
  - 1500 — Equipment
    - 1510 — Accumulated Depreciation
- 2000 — Liabilities
  - 2010 — Accounts Payable
  - 2020 — Credit Card Payable
  - 2030 — Loan Payable
- 3000 — Equity
  - 3010 — Owner's Equity
- 4000 — Income
  - 4010 — Consulting Income
    - 4011 — Consulting: East Coast
    - 4012 — Consulting: West Coast
  - 4020 — Speaking Engagements
    - 4021 — Speaking: East Coast
    - 4022 — Speaking: West Coast
  - 4030 — Book Sales
- 5000 — Expenses
  - 5010 — Advertising
  - 5020 — Car & Truck Expenses
  - 5030 — Contract Labor
  - 5040 — Insurance
  - 5050 — Legal & Professional Fees
  - 5060 — Office Expenses
  - 5070 — Rent
    - 5071 — Rent: Detroit Office
    - 5072 — Rent: Phoenix Office
  - 5080 — Repairs & Maintenance
  - 5090 — Supplies
  - 5100 — Taxes & Licenses
  - 5110 — Travel
    - 5111 — Travel: Business Development
    - 5112 — Travel: Conferences
  - 5200 — Payroll
    - 5210 — Payroll: Sales Team
    - 5220 — Payroll: Operations Team
  - 5300 — Meals & Entertainment
  - 5400 — Utilities
  - 5500 — Wages
  - 5600 — Other Expenses

Different industries have unique tracking needs that should be reflected in your chart of accounts:

- Retail businesses need detailed inventory tracking, cost of goods sold categories, and potentially seasonal revenue accounts.
- Service businesses might focus more on labor costs, project-based revenue tracking, and professional development expenses.
- Manufacturing companies require complex cost of goods sold tracking, including raw materials, direct labor, and manufacturing overhead.
- Real estate businesses need separate tracking for each property, including rental income, property taxes, maintenance, and depreciation.

Best Practices for Chart of Accounts Setup

Keep It Simple (But Not Too Simple)

While detail is important, avoid creating so many accounts that your chart becomes confusing. Here's a good rule of thumb: if an account doesn't help you make better business decisions, you probably don't need to list it.

Use Numbering Systems

Many accounting systems allow you to assign numbers to accounts, which helps with organization and reporting. A typical numbering system might look like:

- **1000-1999:** Assets
- **2000-2999:** Liabilities
- **3000-3999:** Equity
- **4000-4999:** Income
- **5000-5999:** Cost of Goods Sold
- **6000-8999:** Expenses

Plan for Growth

Set up your chart of accounts with future expansion in mind. Leave room in your numbering system for new accounts and think about how your business might evolve over the next few years.

Review and Refine Regularly

Your chart of accounts isn't set in stone. As your business grows and changes, review your account structure quarterly or annually. Add new accounts when you identify new tracking needs and consolidate accounts that aren't providing useful information.

Common Mistakes to Avoid

Over-complicating from the start: Don't create dozens of sub-accounts before you understand your actual tracking needs.

Using unclear account names: Avoid vague terms like "Miscellaneous" or "Other" as these become catch-alls that reduce the usefulness of your financial reports.

Ignoring tax implications: Always consider how your account structure will impact tax preparation and compliance.

Inconsistent categorization: Train everyone who enters data to use accounts consistently or else your reports will be messy and meaningless.

Your Foundation for Success

A well-designed chart of accounts makes monthly reporting easier, tax preparation smoother, and strategic decision-making more informed.

> **REMEMBER:** *Your chart of accounts is more than just an organizational tool. It's the foundation that drives other aspects of financial management in your business.*

Take the time to set it up thoughtfully from the beginning. Your future self (and your accountant) will thank you when you're making data-driven decisions with confidence instead of guessing about your business financial performance.

The few minutes you invest in properly structuring your chart of accounts will pay dividends every single month as you generate reports, analyze trends, and steer your business toward greater profitability and success.

I thought it might be helpful for you to see exactly how this works in real life, so I went the extra mile to put together a complimentary set of short, step-by-step video tutorials to walk you through bookkeeping basics from setting up your software to reading your first financial report.

Watch them free at: www.triedandtruefs.com/videotutorials

Activation #1

Accounting 101

Your journey from financial confusion to financial clarity starts right here, right now. Let's set up the systems that will change how you see your business forever—without the overwhelm.

ACTION #1

Connect Bank and Credit Card Accounts

Online banking, or bank feeds, save time so you don't have to enter everything manually. Once you connect your accounts, most transactions will be downloaded and categorized.

> **REMEMBER:** *You're headed from financial confusion to financial clarity without the overwhelm!*

1. Connect a bank or credit card account

   You can connect as many business accounts as you want.

2. Download recent transactions

   Your software should electronically download transactions so that you don't have to enter them manually. Every financial institution is different, so you have to pay close attention to confirm that all transactions have come in from the beginning date that you plan on tracking. If this does not happen, you have two options:

1. **Export the data from your online bank account and import it to the accounting system:**
    a. Log on to your online bank account
    b. Download transactions for the date range you need into a "CSV" file
    c. Save in your preferred location
    d. Upload the transaction file in your accounting system

2. **Manually enter the missing transactions:**
    a. Click +New
    b. Select your transaction type
    c. Enter details

    Pro Tip: Every time you log on to your accounting system, be sure to refresh the bank feed to ensure that all of your most recent transactions have come in.

    - Go to Bank transactions
    - Select Update

❸ The Tax Form Strategy: Your Secret Weapon

Your final step in this section is to verify that each expense category that is listed on your tax form is listed on your chart of accounts. If you find one that you will likely need that is not listed, simply add it.

- Go to Chart of accounts
- Select New
- Enter the account category (the way it's listed on your tax form)
- Select "expenses" from the Account type dropdown
- Select the appropriate category from the Detail type dropdown
- Select Save

4

Categorizing Transactions Like a Pro

• Training your system for automated accuracy •

The Art of Transaction Categorization

Now that your business accounts are connected and transactions are flowing automatically into your accounting system, you've reached the most critical phase of bookkeeping: ensuring every transaction lands in the right category. This isn't just about organization. Proper categorization is the foundation for accurate financial reporting, meaningful business insights, and strategic decision-making. It just is!

Think of transaction categorization as teaching your accounting system to speak your business language. The better you train it, the more valuable insights it will provide about your spending patterns, profitability by category, and opportunities for cost optimization.

Understanding AI-Powered Suggestions

Modern accounting software comes equipped with artificial intelligence that analyzes transaction details to suggest appropriate categories. This AI examines several data points to make its recommendations.

What the AI Analyzes

Vendor Names: The system recognizes common vendors and suggests categories based on typical purchases. For example, transactions from "Staples" might automatically suggest "Office Supplies."

Transaction Descriptions: Keywords in the bank description help identify transaction types. Terms like "fuel" might automatically suggest "car & truck" or "repairs and maintenance."

Transaction Amounts: Consistent amounts might indicate recurring expenses like rent, loan payments, or subscriptions.

Historical Patterns: As you correct and confirm categorizations, the AI learns your preferences and becomes more accurate over time.

Industry Standards: The system applies general business knowledge about how similar businesses typically categorize expenses.

As powerful as these AI-driven tools already are, they continue to evolve at an extraordinary pace. Each year accounting software becomes smarter, faster, and more intuitive, reducing manual work and helping business owners make better financial decisions. While no system is perfect and your oversight is still essential, the future of bookkeeping is undeniably shifting toward deeper automation and predictive insights. Staying informed about these rapid developments ensures you not only keep your books accurate today, but you also remain ready to take advantage of tomorrow's innovations.

The Learning Curve Reality

While AI suggestions are helpful, they're not perfect, especially in the beginning. The system doesn't understand your specific business model, unique vendor relationships, or strategic categorization preferences. This is why reviewing the categories before you post the transaction is crucial for long-term efficiency.

The Training Phase

Commit to the Process. During your first few months, plan to spend extra time on transaction review. This upfront investment pays enormous dividends later when your system accurately categorizes 80 to 90% of transactions automatically.

Week 1–2:	Expect to manually review and correct most transactions
Month 1–2:	AI accuracy improves to 60 to 70% as it learns your patterns and you set up "rules"
Month 3–6:	Well-trained systems achieve 80 to 90% accuracy
Ongoing:	Minimal manual intervention needed for routine transactions

Best Practices for Training

Be Consistent: Always categorize similar transactions the same way. If you categorize Amazon purchases as "Office Supplies" once, do that every time (unless the purchase is genuinely different).

Don't Rush: Take time to read transaction descriptions and vendor names carefully. Quick, careless categorization trains the AI incorrectly.

Use Specific Categories: Instead of lumping everything into "General Expenses," use specific categories (or sub-categories) that provide meaningful insights.

Document Your Decisions: Keep notes about why you categorize certain vendors or transaction types in specific ways, especially for unusual situations.

Setting Up Powerful Automation Rules

Rules are your secret weapon for transaction categorization efficiency. These automated instructions tell your accounting system exactly how to handle specific types of transactions without wasting your precious time every month.

Common Rule Categories

Vendor-Based Rules: Automatically categorize all transactions from specific vendors

- Amazon ➔ Office Supplies
- Office Depot ➔ Office Supplies
- Chevron ➔ Fuel/Vehicle Expenses
- Verizon ➔ Telecommunications

Amount-Based Rules: Handle recurring payments with consistent amounts

- $1,200 monthly payment ➔ Rent & Lease
- $89.99 monthly payment ➔ Software Subscriptions
- $350 quarterly payment ➔ Business Insurance

Description-Based Rules: Categorize based on keywords in transaction descriptions

- Contains "PAYROLL" ➔ Payroll Expenses
- Contains "INSURANCE" ➔ Insurance
- Contains "FUEL" ➔ Vehicle Expenses
- Contains "ATM" ➔ Bank Fees

Combination Rules: Use multiple criteria for precise categorization

- Vendor = "Amazon" AND Amount < $50 ➔ Office Supplies
- Vendor = "Amazon" AND Amount > $500 ➔ Equipment

Strategic Rule Implementation

Start Simple: Begin with your most frequent, obvious transactions. Don't try to create rules for every possible scenario immediately.

Test and Refine: Monitor how your rules perform and adjust them as needed. A rule that seemed logical might create unexpected categorizations.

Avoid Over-Automation: Don't create rules for transactions that might legitimately fall into different categories. Amazon purchases, for example, might be office supplies, equipment, or inventory, depending on what you buy.

Regular Audits: Review your rules quarterly to ensure they still make sense as your business evolves.

Advanced Categorization Strategies

Multi-Purpose Vendor Handling

Some vendors provide multiple types of goods or services, requiring more sophisticated approaches. In these cases, create sub-categories. For example, instead of one "Amazon" rule, use:

- Amazon Office Supplies
- Amazon Equipment
- Amazon Inventory

Use Transaction Amounts as Guides

- Small amounts (under $100) might be office supplies
- Large amounts (over $500) might be equipment purchases
- Medium amounts might require manual review

Seasonal Considerations

- Your categorization might change based on business cycles or seasonal needs.

Project-Based Categorization

For project-driven businesses, consider categorizing by project classification.

- **Client Projects:** Track expenses by specific client work

- **Internal Projects:** Separate R&D, marketing campaigns, and operational improvements

- **Geographic Regions:** For businesses operating in multiple locations

Tax Optimization Categories

Structure categories to align with tax deductions and reporting requirements.

- **Separate Business Meals:** Keep client entertainment separate from employee meals
- **Home Office Expenses:** Track qualified home office deductions separately
- **Professional Development:** Distinguish between training, conferences, and certifications
- **Travel Categories:** Separate local travel, out-of-state travel, and international travel

Common Categorization Mistakes to Avoid

The "Miscellaneous" Trap

Avoid using "Miscellaneous" or "Other" categories as catch-alls. These categories provide no meaningful insights and often hide important spending patterns.

Inconsistent Personal vs. Business

Be strict about what constitutes a business expense. When in doubt, consult with your accountant rather than guessing.

Over-Complicated Categories

Don't create so many categories that the system becomes unwieldy. If a category will only have a few transactions per year, consider consolidating it with a broader category.

Timing Issues

Ensure recurring transactions (like rent or loan payments) are categorized consistently each month, even if the vendor name or description varies slightly.

The Professional Efficiency Payoff

Monthly Routine Efficiency

Once your system is well-trained, the time spent will normalize.

Daily: 5 – 10 minutes to approve obvious, correctly categorized transactions

Weekly: 10 – 15 minutes to review and correct any mis-categorizations

Monthly: 30 minutes for final review and reconciliation

Meaningful Financial Reports

Proper categorization enables powerful business insights:

- **Expense Analysis:** Identify which categories are growing or shrinking
- **Vendor Analysis:** Understand your largest expense relationships
- **Trend Identification:** Spot seasonal patterns or unusual spending
- **Budget Comparison:** Compare actual spending to budgeted amounts by category
- **Tax Preparation:** Generate accurate reports for tax deduction substantiation

Strategic Decision Support

Well-categorized data supports important business decisions:

- **Cost Reduction:** Identify categories for potential savings
- **Vendor Negotiations:** Use spending data to negotiate better terms
- **Pricing Strategies:** Understand true costs to improve pricing
- **Investment Planning:** Track ROI (return on investment) on different types of business investments

Maintaining Your Categorization System

Regular System Maintenance

- **Monthly Reviews:** Check for new vendors or transaction types that need rules
- **Quarterly Audits:** Ensure existing rules are still working correctly
- **Annual Cleanup:** Archive old vendors and update categories for tax changes

Team Training

Take these steps if multiple people handle transaction categorization:

- Create written guidelines for categorization decisions
- Establish approval processes for new categories or rules
- Conduct regular training sessions on proper categorization

Continuous Improvement

Help your categorization system evolve with your business:

- Add new categories for new business activities
- Refine existing categories for better insights
- Update rules as vendor patterns change
- Adjust for new tax requirements or business structures

The Professional Standard

Categorizing transactions like a pro means creating a system that works automatically, provides meaningful insights, and supports strategic business decisions. The initial investment in training your system and setting up smart rules pays dividends in time savings, financial clarity, and business intelligence without the overwhelm.

> **REMEMBER:** *Every properly categorized transaction is an investment in your business financial intelligence.*

The more accurately you train your system today, the more valuable insights it will provide tomorrow, enabling you to make informed decisions that drive profitability and growth.

Activation #2

FinancialCPR™

In this section, we explore the importance of tracking and analyzing your spending trends. As a business owner, it is essential to have a clear understanding of your goals and financials, including where your money is going and how it is being spent. By tracking your spending and analyzing your trends, you can identify areas where you can cut costs, reduce waste, and improve your bottom line without the overwhelm that normally accompanies these decisions.

ACTION #2

Categorize and Post Your Transactions

The artificial intelligence (AI) in your accounting software will auto-categorize some of your transactions based on the memo description from your financial institution. Once your transactions are downloaded, you'll need to review them to ensure they are accurate before you post them.

❶ Download the latest bank and credit card transactions

For most banks, your software provider is allowed to download the latest available transactions every night around 10 p.m. PT. Some may take a little longer. You can also manually "update" your accounts anytime to get the latest available transactions.

- Go to Bank transactions
- Select Update

Pro Tip: If you see a message about additional authentication, follow the on-screen steps to continue the update. Not all banks require this, but some do for added security. This is very important and should not be ignored.

This updates all of your bank and credit card accounts.

❷ Review and categorize downloaded transactions

1. From the Bank transactions window, select the title for the account you want to review.

2. Make sure you are on the "For review" tab to start your review.

3. Review the transactions and categories listed and select "Post" if they are accurate.

4. If they need to be adjusted, simply click the transaction to open it and begin your edits. Your software sends downloaded transactions to the For Review tab. Review them one by one.

   For each transaction, you have the option to match, add, or view multiple matches. Follow the steps in the section for each option:

   - Match with an existing transaction
   - Confirm paired bank transfers View and review multiple matches
   - View images for check transactions Add a new transaction

   The only transfers you should pair are the ones where both accounts are connected to your accounting system. If both are not connected, change the transaction type to "categorize" rather than "transfer."

Pro Tip: AI can automatically match (and post) transactions by creating "rules" for the system to follow. You will see that functionality on the transaction once you open it up.

❸ Review matched or added transactions

After you match (post or add) downloaded transactions, they're recorded onto your "bank register." You can review your work and make sure everything is correct in the Categorized or Excluded tab. It's a good idea to quickly check this after your review:

1. Go to Bank transactions
2. Select the tile for the account you want to review
3. Go to the Categorized or Excluded tab
4. Select the link in the Added or Matched column to review the transaction

Pro Tip: If you need to change or move a transaction to a different account, undo or unmatch it first. Make all of your changes before you do your month-end reconciliation.

5

The Reconciliation Process

• Amateur bookkeeping vs. professional financial management •

The Great Misconception

Picture this: you've purchased your accounting software, connected all your business accounts, and diligently categorized and accepted every transaction that flows through your system. You sit back with satisfaction, thinking your bookkeeping is complete. Then you run your first financial report and something feels . . . off. The numbers don't match what you expected, or even worse, they don't match your bank statements.

Welcome to the most common misconception in small business bookkeeping: thinking that automation equals completion. While technology has revolutionized how we track financial data, it hasn't eliminated the need for human oversight and verification. This is where the reconciliation process begins. This is a crucial step that separates amateur bookkeeping from professional financial management.

Why Reconciliation Gets Overlooked

The oversight happens because modern accounting software makes the initial steps feel so seamless. Transactions download automatically, artificial intelligence suggests categories, and with a few clicks, everything appears organized and complete. This technological efficiency creates a false sense of security, leading many business owners to believe their work is done.

But here's the reality: automated systems, while powerful, are not infallible. Bank feeds can miss transactions, duplicate entries can occur, timing differences create discrepancies, and human errors in categorization can compound over time. Without reconciliation, these small issues snowball into significant financial reporting problems that can mislead business decisions and create compliance issues.

The Power of Three: A Simple Framework

Three is my favorite number for many reasons, but primarily because it's easy to remember and implement three things consistently. When it comes to managing your accounting records effectively, I recommend a simple three-step FinancialCPR™ approach that ensures accuracy and completeness: Categorize (or Code), Post, and Reconcile transactions each month.

Step 1: Categorize Your Transactions (covered in chapter 4)

This involves reviewing every transaction that flows into your accounting system and ensuring it's assigned to the appropriate account category. Even with AI assistance, human oversight ensures transactions land in the most strategic categories for your business analysis needs.

Step 2: Post Your Transactions (also covered in chapter 4)

Posting means officially recording transactions in your accounting system, moving them from "pending" or "for review" status to permanent entries in your financial records. This step confirms that all transactions are captured and properly dated.

Step 3: Reconcile Your Transactions

This is where you match your accounting records against external statements like bank statements, credit card statements, and other financial institution records. Reconciliation ensures that what your accounting system shows matches what actually happened in your bank accounts.

Only after completing all three steps can you confidently say you have balanced books. Even then, your work isn't finished.

The Triple-Check Principle

When dealing with technology, systems, numbers, and financial data, you should always triple check your work. Numbers have a way of revealing inconsistencies that may not be apparent during the initial review, and the cost of financial errors far outweighs the time invested in verification.

After completing your reconciliation, the triple-check involves running your three critical financial reports and examining the entries to ensure everything is in its proper place. This final verification step catches any remaining discrepancies and confirms the accuracy of your financial data.

The Critical Nature of Reconciliation

Reconciliation serves five crucial functions that extend far beyond simple accuracy verification:

1. **Error Detection and Correction**

   Bank feeds occasionally miss transactions, especially electronic transfers, automatic payments, or transactions that occur near month-end. Reconciliation identifies these gaps, ensuring your financial records are complete.

2. **Fraud Prevention**

   Regular reconciliation helps identify unauthorized transactions, duplicate charges, or suspicious activity. The sooner you catch fraudulent activity, the better your chances of recovering funds and preventing future occurrences.

3. **Timing Difference Resolution**

   Checks written but not yet cashed, deposits made but not yet cleared, and automatic payments with different processing dates create timing differences between your records and bank statements. Reconciliation accounts for these differences and ensures accurate cash position reporting.

4. **Data Integrity Verification**

   Technology glitches can cause transaction duplication, incorrect amounts, or categorization errors. Reconciliation serves as a quality control checkpoint that maintains the integrity of your financial data.

5. **Compliance and Audit Preparation**

   Reconciled accounts provide the documentation trail necessary for tax preparation, loan applications, and potential audits. Lenders and auditors expect to see regular reconciliation documentation as proof of sound financial management.

The Three Critical Reports for Your Financial Health

After reconciliation, running and reviewing your three critical reports provides a comprehensive view of your business financial health.

1. **The Profit & Loss Statement**

   This report shows your business profitability over a specific period, revealing whether your operations are generating profit or creating losses. After reconciliation, review this report to ensure the following:

   - All income sources are captured and properly categorized
   - Expense categories reflect actual business spending
   - The time period covered matches your analysis needs
   - Unusual or unexpected amounts are investigated and explained

2. **The Balance Sheet**

   Your balance sheet provides a snapshot of your business financial position, showing assets, liabilities, and equity at a specific point in time. Post-reconciliation review should confirm the following:

   - Bank account balances match your actual account balances
   - Accounts receivable accurately reflects money customers owe
   - Accounts payable correctly shows money you owe vendors
   - Asset and liability accounts are properly valued and classified

3. **The Cash Flow Statement**

   This report tracks how cash moves through your business, showing the sources and uses of cash during a specific period. After reconciliation, verify the following:

- Operating activities reflect actual business cash generation
- Investing activities accurately capture asset purchases and sales
- Financing activities properly show borrowing and debt payments
- The ending cash position matches your reconciled bank balances

Finding Your Reconciliation Frequency Rhythm

The frequency of your reconciliation depends on your business activity level and complexity. Depending on the volume of activity and the stage you are in with your business, you will be able to find your rhythm. Here are a few things to consider.

Monthly Reconciliation (Recommended Standard)

For most businesses, monthly reconciliation provides the optimal balance between accuracy and efficiency. Monthly reconciliation affords these opportunities:

- Catch and correct errors before they compound
- Maintain current and accurate financial reports
- Meet most lender and investor reporting requirements
- Support timely business decision-making

Quarterly Reconciliation (Minimum Acceptable)

Businesses with lower transaction volumes might reconcile quarterly, but this should be considered the absolute minimum frequency. Quarterly reconciliation increases these risks:

- Larger error accumulation requiring more time to resolve
- Outdated financial information affecting business decisions
- Difficulty remembering transaction details for older items
- Potential compliance issues with more frequent reporting requirements

Weekly or Daily Reconciliation (High-Activity Businesses)

Businesses with high transaction volumes, multiple bank accounts, or critical cash flow timing might benefit from more frequent reconciliation. For example:

- Retail businesses with daily cash deposits
- Service businesses with rapid customer payment cycles
- Companies with complex multi-location operations
- Businesses operating on thin cash flow margins

Making Your Reconciliation Process Systematic

Effective reconciliation requires a systematic approach that becomes routine and efficient over time:

Preparation Phase

Gather all necessary statements and reports, ensure your accounting system is current, and set aside uninterrupted time for the process.

Comparison Phase

Methodically compare each transaction on your bank statement with corresponding entries in your accounting system, marking off matched items.

Investigation Phase

Research and resolve any discrepancies, missing transactions, or timing differences identified during comparison.

Adjustment Phase

Make necessary adjusting entries to correct errors or account for legitimate timing differences.

Documentation Phase

Record your reconciliation work, maintaining supporting documentation for future reference and audit purposes.

The Professional Payoff

Mastering the reconciliation process transforms you from someone who "does bookkeeping" to someone who "manages finances professionally." This distinction matters in these cases:

- Applying for business loans or credit lines
- Attracting investors or potential buyers
- Managing cash flow during challenging periods
- Making strategic business decisions based on accurate data
- Preparing for tax season or potential audits

Regular reconciliation gives you peace of mind because your financial reports accurately reflect reality—not guesses. And when you pair reconciliation with intentional cash allocation through the P.O.T.S.™ method (Payroll, Operating Expenses, Taxes, and Savings), you go a step further. You're not just confirming what happened—you're making sure your money is sitting where it needs to be. Reconciliation tells you the truth; P.O.T.S.™ ensures you respond to that truth wisely by keeping funds set aside for the things that matter most.

This combination leads to better decision-making, improved cash flow management, and stronger trust with financial institutions and business partners. Reconciliation may not be the most exciting part of business ownership, but it's the discipline that keeps your financial foundation solid. In the complex world of business finance, reconciliation is what keeps everything in balance—and P.O.T.S.™ makes sure that balance has purpose.

Activation #3

Reconciliation:
What It Means and Why It Matters

In this section, we will provide you with step-by-step guidance on how to reconcile your business accounts, as well as provide tips and best practices to help you stay on top of your financials.

ACTION #3

Reconcile Transactions

When you have your bank statement in hand, compare each transaction with the ones entered in your accounting system. If everything matches, you know your accounts are balanced and accurate. We recommend reconciling your checking, savings, and credit card accounts every month, but no less than quarterly. Here's how to get started.

1. Review your opening balance

   If you're reconciling an account for the first time, review the opening balance to ensure it is accurate. It needs to match the balance of your real-life bank account for the day you decided to start tracking transactions. If the opening balance is not accurate, you can go to the chart of accounts, click "view register," locate "opening balance equity" and correct the amount.

2. Start a reconciliation

   Once you have your monthly bank or credit card statement, you can start reconciling.

1. Select Reconcile. If you're reconciling for the very first time, select Get started to continue.

2. From the Account ▼ dropdown, select the account you want to reconcile. Make sure it's the same one on your statement.

3. Review the Beginning balance. Make sure the beginning balance in your software matches the one on your statement.

4. Enter the Ending balance and Ending date on your statement. Some banks call the ending balance a "new balance" or a "closing balance."

5. If you see it, review the Last statement ending date. This is the end date of your last reconciliation. Your current bank statement should start the day after.

6. When you're ready to start, select Start reconciling.

Pro Tip: If you're reconciling multiple months, do them one month at a time, starting with your oldest statement.

❸ Compare your statement with your accounting software

Now, simply compare the transactions on your statement with what's in your software system. Go over them one-by-one. The tricky part is making sure you have the right dates and transactions so you know everything matches.

Next steps: Review past reconciliations

Run a reconciliation report to review your work:

1. Go to Bookkeeping or Accounting, then select Reconcile.
2. Select History by account.
3. Use the dropdown menus to select the account and date range.

Edit completed reconciliations

You can make changes to past reconciliations, but be careful. Changes can unbalance your accounts and other reconciliations. They also can affect the beginning balance of your next reconciliation.

6

Finding and Fixing Errors

• Building confidence through accurate financial records •

Overcoming the Fear Factor

One of the biggest obstacles preventing business owners from maintaining accurate books is the paralyzing fear of "breaking something" in their accounting system. This fear keeps many entrepreneurs from making necessary corrections, allowing small errors to compound into significant financial reporting problems over time.

Let me put your mind at ease with this fundamental truth: **things can always be fixed.**

Accounting software is designed to track changes, maintain audit trails, and allow corrections. The risk of permanently damaging your financial records through normal adjustments is virtually zero. The real risk lies in leaving errors uncorrected, which can lead to poor business decisions based on inaccurate financial information.

Think of error correction as financial housekeeping. Regular maintenance keeps your business running smoothly rather than creating the need for emergency repairs that become necessary when problems are ignored.

The Power of the Three Critical Reports

Your three critical reports, P&L, Balance Sheet, and Cash Flow Statement (General Ledger), serve as your error detection system. These reports reveal inconsistencies, unusual patterns, and obvious mistakes that might not be apparent when reviewing individual transactions. Here's what to look for in each report.

Profit & Loss Statement Red Flags

- Expenses appearing in income categories or vice versa
- Unusually high amounts in typically small expense categories
- Round numbers that seem too convenient (often indicating estimates rather than actual transactions)
- Negative amounts in categories that should always be positive
- Seasonal expenses appearing in wrong time periods

Profit & Loss Statement

For Year Ended Dec 31, 20XX

INCOME	
Consulting Income	$85,000
Speaking Engagements	$25,000
Book Sales	$-5,000
Total Income	$105,000
EXPENSES	
Advertising	$3,000
Car & Truck Expenses	$2,200
Contract Labor	$8,000
Depreciation	$1,500
Insurance	$2,500
Legal & Professional Fees	$4,000
Office Expenses	$1,800
Rent	$12,000
Repairs & Maintenance	$900
Supplies	$1,500
Taxes & Licenses	$1,800
Travel	$3,500
Meals & Entertainment	$2,500
Utilities	$2,700
Wages	$20,000
Other Expenses	$-500
Total Expenses	$67,400
NET PROFIT	$37,600

Negative income — may signal misclassification

Round number — may be estimate

Unusually high — investigate

Negative expense — check for errors

Example created by Valaise Smith, 2025

Balance Sheet Warning Signs

- Asset accounts with negative balances (except accumulated depreciation)
- Liability accounts with positive balances when they should be negative
- Bank account balances that don't match your actual account balances
- Accounts receivable amounts that don't align with outstanding customer invoices
- Accounts payable that don't reflect what you actually owe vendors

Balance Sheet
As of Dec 31, 20XX

ASSETS		
Cash	$-2,000	← Negative cash flow
Accounts Receivable	$15,000	← May not match invoices
Prepaid Expenses	$3,000	
Equipment	$25,000	
Accumulated Depreciation	$-5,000	
Inventory	$8,000	
Total Assets	**$44,000**	
LIABILITIES		
Accounts Payable	$12,000	← May not match actual owed
Credit Card Payable	$3,500	
Loan Payable	$-15,000	← Positive vs. negative sign issue
Total Liabilities	**$500**	
EQUITY		
Owner's Equity	$28,000	
Total Equity	**$28,000**	
Total Liabilities & Equity	**$28,500**	

Example created by Valaise Smith, 2025

Cash Flow Statement Anomalies

- Large unexplained changes in cash position
- Operating activities that don't align with P&L results
- Missing loan payments or asset purchases
- Inconsistent patterns compared to previous periods

Cash Flow Statement
For Year Ended Dec 31, 20XX

OPERATING ACTIVITIES		
Net Income	$15,000	
Depreciation	$5,000	
Change in Accounts Receivable	$-7,000	
Change in Accounts Payable	$4,000	
Other Adjustments	$-12,000	← Large unexplained adjustment
Net Cash from Operating	**$5,000**	← Doesn't align with P&L results
INVESTING ACTIVITIES		
Purchase of Equipment	$0	← No asset purchase recorded
Other Investing	$-2,000	
Net Cash from Investing	**$-2,000**	
FINANCING ACTIVITIES		
Loan Proceeds	$10,000	
Loan Payments	$0	← Missing loan payments
Owner Contributions	$5,000	
Net Cash from Financing	**$15,000**	
Net Increase (Decrease) in Cash	**$18,000**	

Example created by Valaise Smith, 2025

Simple Transaction Category Corrections

The most common errors, and fortunately the easiest to fix, involve transactions landing in the wrong categories. These mistakes happen frequently during the initial setup period when your accounting system is still learning your business patterns.

The Safe Correction Process

Step 1: Locate the Transaction - Find the incorrectly categorized transaction through your banking or transaction center within your accounting software.

Step 2: Edit the Category - Open the transaction and simply change the category assignment from the incorrect account to the correct one.

Step 3: Verify the Amount - Ensure the dollar amount remains unchanged. This is crucial because altering amounts can affect previous reconciliations and create additional complications.

Step 4: Save and Confirm - Save the changes and verify that the transaction now appears in the correct category on your reports.

Why Amount Changes Matter

As long as you only change the category assignment without altering the dollar amount, your previous reconciliations remain intact. This is because reconciliation matches the total dollar amounts between your accounting system and bank statements. The specific categorization doesn't affect this matching process.

However, if you change transaction amounts, you risk throwing your reconciliations out of balance, requiring additional adjustments to maintain accuracy.

The Chart of Accounts Reconciliation Check

One of the most powerful but often overlooked error detection methods involves systematically reviewing your chart of accounts for reconciliation status indicators. This process reveals duplicate transactions, unnecessary entries, and reconciliation issues that can significantly impact your financial accuracy.

Understanding the Status Indicators

Modern accounting systems use specific indicators to show the reconciliation status of each transaction:

- "R" **(Reconciled):** The transaction has been matched to a bank statement and confirmed as accurate. This is what you want to see for all bank-connected transactions.
- "C" **(Cleared):** The transaction has been marked as cleared but not fully reconciled. This often indicates a timing difference or partial matching.
- **Blank:** No reconciliation status has been assigned, suggesting the transaction may be duplicate, manually entered when it shouldn't have been, or missed during reconciliation.

The Systematic Review Process

Step 1: Generate Chart of Accounts Report — Run a detailed chart of accounts report that shows individual transactions with their reconciliation status.

Step 2: Focus on Connected - Accounts — Pay particular attention to accounts that have bank feeds connected like checking accounts, savings accounts, and credit card accounts.

Step 3: Investigate Anomalies — For every account showing a blank or "C" status indicator:

- Verify the transaction actually occurred by checking bank statements
- Determine if it's a duplicate of an already-reconciled transaction
- Assess whether it should have been manually entered

Step 4: Take Corrective Action

- Delete duplicate transactions
- Reconcile legitimate transactions that were missed
- Adjust or reclassify transactions as appropriate

Common Scenarios Requiring Correction

Duplicate Transactions: These often occur when both automatic bank feeds and manual entry create records for the same transaction. Keep the automatically imported transaction and delete the manual entry.

Manual Entries for Bank Feed Transactions: Sometimes users manually enter transactions that later import through bank feeds, creating duplicates with different reconciliation statuses.

Timing Differences: Transactions can appear in your accounting system but haven't yet appeared on bank statements, or vice versa.

Bank Feed Errors: Occasionally, bank feeds import incorrect amounts or duplicate transactions. These require manual correction.

The Strategic Value of Clean Books

Maintaining accurate, error-free financial records isn't just about compliance or appeasing your accountant, it's about empowering strategic business decisions with reliable data.

The Value of Decision-Making Confidence

When you trust your financial reports, you can confidently make decisions such as:

- Pricing strategies based on accurate cost analysis
- Investment opportunities supported by reliable cash flow projections
- Operational changes guided by precise expense tracking
- Growth initiatives backed by solid financial foundations

The Value of Performance Monitoring

Clean books enable accurate performance measurement.

- Month-to-month comparisons reveal true trends
- Budget variance analysis identifies real issues
- Profitability analysis guides resource allocation
- Cash flow forecasting prevents financial surprises

The Value of Professional Credibility

Accurate financial records enhance your professional reputation with key relationships:

- Lenders who require reliable financial statements for credit decisions
- Investors who need trustworthy data for investment evaluations
- Business partners who depend on accurate reporting for their partnership reporting
- Accountants who can work more efficiently with clean data for strategic advice

Establishing an Error-Correction Routine

Make error detection and correction a regular part of your financial management routine.

Weekly Quick Scans: Spend 15 minutes reviewing recent transactions for obvious categorization errors.

Monthly Deep Reviews: Conduct thorough reviews of all three critical reports and chart of accounts reconciliation status.

Quarterly Clean-Up: Perform comprehensive error detection and correction, focusing on annual trends and patterns.

Annual System Audits: Review your entire chart of accounts structure and reconciliation processes for optimization opportunities.

REMEMBER: *The goal isn't perfection, it's continuous improvement. Each error you find and fix makes your financial data more reliable and your business decisions more informed. The confidence that comes from knowing your books accurately reflect your business reality is invaluable for both day-to-day operations and long-term strategic planning.*

7

Creating Monthly Routines

• Building consistency for lasting financial success •

The Power of Working "On" Your Business

As business owners, we often find ourselves trapped in the daily grind of working "in" the business, responding to customer needs, putting out fires, and handling immediate operational demands. While these activities are essential, they can consume all our time and energy, leaving little room for the strategic activities that actually grow and strengthen our businesses.

Financial management falls squarely in the "working on your business" category. It's the behind-the-scenes work that provides the insights and control necessary to make informed decisions, identify opportunities, and avoid potential pitfalls. Yet because it doesn't generate immediate revenue or solve urgent customer problems, bookkeeping often gets pushed to the bottom of our priority list.

This is where the power of routine comes in. By establishing a consistent monthly practice, you transform financial management from an overwhelming, catch-up activity into a manageable, strategic business function.

FinancialCPR™: Keeping Your Business Healthy

Just as CPR can save a life in medical emergencies, FinancialCPR™ can save your business from financial distress. Remember our three-step approach from chapters 4 and 5? Categorize, Post, and Reconcile—CPR for your finances. This isn't just a clever acronym. It represents the life sustaining rhythm your business needs to maintain financial health.

Why FinancialCPR™ Matters

In the medical field, CPR is consistent chest compressions to maintain blood flow to vital organs. With FinancialCPR™, consistent monthly routines maintain accurate data flow to critical business decisions. Just as you can't skip chest compressions during life-saving efforts, you can't skip any of the three CPR steps without compromising your financial health.

Categorize ensures every financial transaction has a proper home, creating meaningful data for analysis. ***Post*** confirms that all transactions are officially recorded and become part of your permanent financial record. ***Reconcile*** verifies that your internal records match external reality, ensuring accuracy and completeness.

When performed consistently each month, FinancialCPR™ becomes the heartbeat of your business operations, a steady, reliable rhythm that keeps everything functioning properly.

The Professional Development Day Strategy

I call my monthly financial routine my "professional development day," and it has been an absolute game-changer for both my business operations and peace of mind. The key to success lies in choosing the right timing, a period when business naturally slows down or when you typically experience lower productivity.

This dedicated time allows you to perform FinancialCPR™ without interruption, ensuring each step receives the attention it deserves. Just as medical professionals practice CPR regularly to maintain proficiency, business owners must practice FinancialCPR™ consistently to maintain accuracy.

Finding Your Optimal Time

End-of-Month Lulls: Many businesses experience natural slowdowns at month-end as customers prepare for new billing cycles or delay decisions until the following month.

Mid-Week Valleys: Tuesdays and Wednesdays often have fewer interruptions than Mondays (catch-up day) or Fridays (wind-down day).

Seasonal Quiet Periods: Every business has predictable slower seasons, use these periods to establish and refine your routines.

Personal Energy Patterns: Consider your own energy cycles. Some people are more analytical in the morning, while others prefer administrative tasks in the afternoon.

Industry-Specific Rhythms: Retail businesses might choose mornings before stores open, while service businesses might prefer times when clients are typically unavailable.

The Training Effect: Building System Intelligence

Think of your monthly routine as "training the brain" of your accounting system. Each month that you consistently perform FinancialCPR™ (categorizing, posting, and reconciling transactions) your software becomes smarter about your business patterns. This artificial intelligence learns your preferences, recognizes your vendors, and anticipates your categorization choices.

The FinancialCPR™ approach creates a feedback loop where each month's consistency improves the next month's efficiency. Your accounting system learns to "breathe" more naturally, requiring less manual intervention over time.

The Compounding Benefits

Month 1 - 3: Establishing the FinancialCPR™ routine feels time-intensive as you correct numerous categorization errors and set up automation rules.

Month 4 - 6: The system begins recognizing patterns, reducing manual corrections by 40 to 50%.

Month 7-12: Well-trained systems achieve 80 to 90% accuracy, transforming your monthly routine from tedious data entry to strategic analysis.

Ongoing: Monthly maintenance becomes a quick review process focused on insights rather than corrections.

Creating Economies of Scale

Consistent monthly FinancialCPR™ routines create operational efficiencies that extend far beyond bookkeeping. When your financial processes are systematized and current, you create economies of scale that benefit multiple aspects of your business.

Streamlined Decision-Making

Current financial data enables faster, more confident business decisions. Instead of guessing about cash flow or profitability, you have real-time insights that support strategic choices.

Reduced Professional Service Costs

Accountants and bookkeepers can work more efficiently with well-maintained records, reducing professional service costs and improving the quality of their advice.

Improved Vendor Relationships

Timely, accurate financial management supports better vendor relationships through on-time payments and clear communication about payment terms.

Enhanced Lending Capabilities

Banks and lenders favor businesses with consistent, current financial records, improving your access to credit and potentially reducing borrowing costs.

Designing Your Monthly FinancialCPR™ Routine

Week 1: Categorize - Setting the Foundation

- Download and review all bank and credit card transactions
- Correct any obvious categorization errors
- Set up new automation rules for recurring vendors
- Ensure every transaction has a proper category assignment

Week 2: Post and Reconcile - Confirming Accuracy

- Post all reviewed transactions to make them permanent records
- Reconcile all connected accounts to bank statements
- Run the three critical reports (P&L, Balance Sheet, and Cash Flow Statement) and review for anomalies
- Investigate and correct any discrepancies or duplicate transactions

Week 3: Analysis and Insights - Using Your FinancialCPR™ Results

- Compare current month to previous months and year-over-year
- Analyze spending patterns and identify optimization opportunities
- Review accounts receivable and payable aging reports

Week 4: Strategic Planning and Documentation - Planning Ahead

- Update financial forecasts based on current data
- Document any process improvements or system changes
- Plan for upcoming financial needs or seasonal adjustments

The Life-Saving Power of Consistency

Just as medical CPR must be performed consistently to be effective, FinancialCPR™ only works when practiced regularly. Skipping months or performing the steps haphazardly reduces effectiveness and can allow financial problems to develop undetected.

The beauty of establishing monthly FinancialCPR™ routines lies in their compound effect. Each month builds upon the previous month's work, creating a snowball effect of accuracy, efficiency, and insight. What initially feels like a significant time investment quickly transforms into a streamlined process that provides disproportionate value relative to the time invested.

Consistency also builds confidence. When you know your books are current and accurate through regular FinancialCPR™, you can make business decisions with certainty rather than hesitation. This confidence translates into better negotiation with vendors, clearer communication with lenders, and more strategic planning for growth opportunities.

Your monthly FinancialCPR™ routine is more than maintaining books. It creates a foundation of financial intelligence that supports every aspect of your business success. The discipline of working "on" your business through consistent financial management pays dividends in improved operations, strategic clarity, and long-term sustainability without the overwhelm.

> **REMEMBER:** *CPR saves lives, and FinancialCPR™ saves businesses. Make it a non-negotiable part of your monthly routine.*

8

Understanding Your Money Flow

• Connecting the dots between your financial statements •

The Financial Statement Symphony

Understanding how money flows through your business is about seeing how all the pieces of your financial puzzle connect to create a complete picture of your business health.

The key to mastering your money flow lies in understanding how different types of transactions flow to different financial reports, and more importantly, how these reports interconnect to give you a comprehensive view of your business performance and position.

The Profit & Loss Statement Is Your Operating Story

Your P&L tells the story of your business operations over a specific period of time. This is where all your income and expense transactions live, showing whether your business activities are generating profit or creating losses.

Income: The Money Coming In

Every dollar your business earns flows through income accounts on your P&L.

Sales Revenue: The primary income from selling your products or services

Service Revenue: Income from providing services to customers

Interest Income: Money earned from business savings or investments

Rental Income: If you rent out business property or equipment

Commission Income: Earnings from referrals or partnerships

Other Income: Miscellaneous business income sources

Expenses: The Money Going Out

All the costs of operating your business appear as expenses on your P&L.

Cost of Goods Sold (COGS): Direct costs to produce your products or deliver services

Operating Expenses: Rent, utilities, insurance, office supplies

Payroll Expenses: Salaries, wages, benefits, payroll taxes

Marketing Expenses: Advertising, promotional materials, website costs

Professional Services: Legal, accounting, consulting fees

Travel and Entertainment: Business-related travel and client entertainment

The Bottom Line Connection

Your P&L ultimately shows your net income (profit) or net loss for the period. This number doesn't just disappear. It flows directly to your Balance Sheet, affecting your overall business equity. Profitable periods increase your equity, while losses decrease it.

The Balance Sheet Is Your Financial Position Snapshot

While your P&L shows performance over time, your Balance Sheet provides a snapshot of your business financial position at a specific moment. It's built on the fundamental accounting equation: Assets = Liabilities + Equity. We looked at these terms in chapter 3, but let's look at them again.

Assets: What Your Business Owns

Assets represent everything of value your business possesses: Current Assets (easily converted to cash within a year):

- Cash and bank account balances
- Accounts receivable; money customers owe you
- Inventory
- Prepaid expenses

Fixed Assets (long-term items)

- Equipment and machinery
- Vehicles
- Real estate
- Furniture and fixtures

Liabilities: What Your Business Owes

Liabilities represent your business financial obligations:

- Current Liabilities (due within a year):

    - Accounts payable; money you owe vendors
    - Credit card balances
    - Short-term loans
    - Accrued expenses
    - Payroll liabilities

- Long-term Liabilities:

    - Mortgages
    - Equipment loans
    - Long-term debt

- Equity — Your Ownership Stake

    Equity represents your ownership interest in the business:

    - Owner's equity or shareholder equity
    - Retained earnings; accumulated profits kept in the business
    - Current year earnings; from your P&L

The Critical Connections: Accounts Receivable and Payable

Two of the most important connections between your operational activities and your financial position involve outstanding invoices and bills. Understanding these connections is crucial for accurate financial reporting and cash flow management.

Accounts Receivable: Money Customers Owe You

When you provide goods or services to customers on credit terms (not requiring immediate payment), you create accounts receivable. Here's how this flows through your financial statements:

The Transaction Process

1. You deliver a product or service to a customer.
2. You create an invoice for the amount owed.
3. The sale appears as income on your P&L.
4. The outstanding invoice appears as accounts receivable on your Balance Sheet.

The Financial Statement Impact:

- P&L Effect: Revenue is recorded when earned, not when cash is received.
- Balance Sheet Effect: Accounts receivable increases your assets.
- Cash Flow Reality: You've made a sale but haven't received cash yet.

Example: You complete a $5,000 consulting project and invoice the client with 30-day payment terms:

- P&L shows $5,000 in service revenue.
- Balance Sheet shows $5,000 in accounts receivable.
- Cash account remains unchanged until payment is received.

Accounts Payable: Money You Owe Vendors

Similarly, when you receive goods or services from vendors and don't pay immediately, you create accounts payable.

The Transaction Process:

1. You receive goods or services from a vendor.
2. The vendor sends you a bill.
3. The expense appears on your P&L.
4. The outstanding bill appears as accounts payable on your Balance Sheet.

The Financial Statement Impact:

- P&L Effect: Expense is recorded when incurred, not when cash is paid.
- Balance Sheet Effect: Accounts payable increases your liabilities.
- Cash Flow Reality: You've incurred an expense but haven't paid cash yet.

Example: You receive a $1,200 utility bill that's due in 30 days:

- P&L shows $1,200 in utility expense.
- Balance Sheet shows $1,200 in accounts payable.
- Cash account remains unchanged until payment is made.

The Importance of Complete Information Entry

To get an accurate picture of your financial position, all financial information must be entered into your accounting system. Partial information leads to incomplete and potentially misleading financial statements.

Why Complete Entry Matters

Accurate Profitability Analysis: If you only record cash transactions, your P&L won't reflect the true profitability of work performed but not yet paid for or expenses incurred but not yet paid.

True Financial Position: Your Balance Sheet can't accurately show your business financial strength if outstanding receivables and payables aren't recorded.

Cash Flow Forecasting: Understanding future cash needs requires knowing when receivables will be collected and when payables must be paid.

Lending and Investment Decisions: Banks and investors need complete financial statements to evaluate your business creditworthiness and potential.

What Must Be Entered

- **All Sales Transactions:** Whether paid immediately or invoiced for later payment
- **All Expense Transactions:** Whether paid immediately or billed for later payment Outstanding Customer
- **Invoices:** All money customers owe you
- **Outstanding Vendor Bills:** All money you owe to suppliers and service providers

- **Asset Purchases:** Equipment, inventory, and other asset acquisitions
- **Loan Transactions:** Both borrowing money and making loan payments

The Flow Between Statements

Understanding how transactions move between financial statements helps you see the complete picture:

From P&L to Balance Sheet

- Net Income from your P&L flows to Retained Earnings on your Balance Sheet.
- Sales on Credit create income on your P&L and Accounts Receivable on your Balance Sheet.
- Expenses on Credit reduce profit on your P&L and create Accounts Payable on your Balance Sheet.

From Balance Sheet to Cash Flow

- Accounts Receivable collections increase cash but don't affect the P&L.
- Accounts Payable payments decrease cash but don't affect the P&L.
- Asset Purchases reduce cash and increase fixed assets, bypassing the P&L.

The Timing Differences

This is why your P&L profit and your cash position can be dramatically different:

- You can be profitable but cash-poor (lots of outstanding receivables).

- You can have negative net income but positive cash flow (collecting old receivables).
- You can show a profit but struggle to pay bills (poor collection of receivables).

Practical Money Flow Management

Monitor Key Relationships

- Accounts Receivable Aging: How quickly customers pay their invoices
- Accounts Payable Aging: How well you're managing vendor payment terms
- Cash Conversion Cycle: Time between paying for inventory and collecting from customers
- Current Ratio: Current assets divided by current liabilities (liquidity measure)

Regular Reconciliation

Monthly reconciliation ensures your accounting records match reality.

- Bank reconciliations verify cash balances.
- Customer statement reconciliations confirm receivable balances.
- Vendor statement reconciliations verify payable amounts.

Cash Flow Forecasting

Use your complete financial information to predict future cash needs.

- When will outstanding receivables be collected?
- When are payables due for payment?
- What upcoming expenses need to be planned for?
- When will seasonal cash flow variations occur?

The Complete Financial Picture

When all transactions are properly recorded, your financial statements work together to tell your complete business story.

- Your P&L shows whether your business model is profitable.
- Your Balance Sheet shows whether your business is financially stable.
- Your Cash Flow Statement shows whether your business can meet its obligations.
- Your Accounts Receivable and Payable reports show the timing of future cash flows.

This complete picture enables informed decision-making about pricing, spending, hiring, expansion, and strategic planning. Without complete information entry, you're essentially flying blind, making critical business decisions based on incomplete or inaccurate data.

Understanding your money flow is more than simply doing routine bookkeeping. When you understand your money flow, you gain the financial intelligence needed to build a sustainable, profitable business that can weather challenges and capitalize on opportunities.

9

Analyzing Your Spending Patterns

• Turning financial data into strategic insights •

The Power of Pattern Recognition

As a business owner, understanding where your money goes is about unlocking the strategic intelligence hidden within your financial data. Your spending patterns tell a story about your business priorities, operational efficiency, and growth potential. The difference between businesses that thrive and those that merely survive often lies in their ability to analyze and act on these patterns.

The magic happens when you step back from individual transactions and see the bigger picture. What feels like random daily expenses suddenly reveals strategic insights when viewed through the lens of comprehensive spending analysis.

The Lightbulb Moment: When Data Meets Reality

One of the most transformative moments in business ownership occurs when you see your actual spending patterns laid out in clear, categorized reports. This revelation often shatters assumptions and illuminates opportunities that were previously invisible. I can't tell you how many clients I have worked with who were amazed when they went through the FinancialCPR™ process and had the opportunity to review their financial statements for the first time!

Common Eye-Opening Discoveries

The Subscription Creep: Many business owners discover they're spending hundreds or thousands of dollars monthly on software subscriptions, many of which are duplicative or underutilized.

The Hidden Cost Centers: Expenses that seem small individually like coffee runs, office supplies, small tools, often add up to significant budget categories when analyzed over time.

The Seasonal Surprises: Businesses often don't realize how dramatically their spending fluctuates seasonally until they see annual patterns in their reports.

The Vendor Concentration: Many discover they're overly dependent on a few expensive vendors, creating both cost and risk management opportunities.

The Category Confusion: What owners think they're spending in marketing versus operations, for example, often differs dramatically from reality when properly categorized and reviewed consistently.

The Three-Perspective Analysis

The most powerful insights come from comparing three different views of your spending:

Mental Assumptions: What you think you're spending in each category

Bank Statement Reality: What individual transactions show

Accounting System Analysis: What comprehensive categorization and reporting reveal

The gaps between these three perspectives often highlight the biggest opportunities for financial optimization.

Essential Spending Pattern Analysis Techniques

Time-Based Analysis

Weekly and Daily Patterns: Understanding daily spending patterns helps optimize cash flow and operational efficiency for many businesses.

Monthly Trending: Comparing spending categories month-over-month identifies patterns, anomalies, and growth trends. Look for categories that are growing faster than your revenue.

Quarterly Patterns: Noticing quarterly rhythms. Many businesses have marketing spends before busy seasons, equipment purchases at year-end, professional services during tax periods.

Year-over-Year Comparison: Comparing annual figures smooths out seasonal fluctuations and reveals true business growth or decline in spending categories.

Category-Based Analysis

Percentage of Revenue Analysis: Calculate each expense category as a percentage of total revenue. This reveals which categories are growing proportionally with your business versus those that might be getting out of control.

Fixed vs. Variable Expense Analysis: Separate your expenses into fixed costs (rent, insurance, loan payments) and variable costs (materials, commission, shipping) to understand your cost structure flexibility.

Discretionary vs. Essential Analysis: Identify which expenses are absolutely necessary for operations versus those that could be reduced or eliminated during tough times.

Vendor-Based Analysis

Top Vendor Analysis: Identify your largest expense relationships. Often 20% of your vendors account for 80% of your spending, creating negotiation opportunities.

Vendor Diversification Review: Assess whether you're too dependent on single vendors for critical business functions, creating potential supply chain risks.

Payment Terms Analysis: Evaluate which vendors offer the best payment terms and whether you're optimizing cash flow through strategic vendor management.

It's one thing to understand where your money is going; it's another to give every dollar a destination before it's spent. That's why earlier in this book we introduced the P.O.T.S.™ Method (Payroll, Operating expenses, Taxes, and Savings). After analyzing your spending patterns, this system helps you put those insights into action. By assigning a set percentage of your revenue to each pot—for example,

40% to payroll, 30% to operating expenses, 20% to taxes, and 10% to savings—you create financial boundaries that align with your goals. It prevents overspending in high-risk categories, ensures taxes are covered before deadlines, and allows you to pay yourself consistently. In short, pairing spending analysis with the P.O.T.S.™ structure doesn't just show you where your money went, it tells your money where to go next.

Strategic Cost Optimization Opportunities

Identifying Cost Reduction Areas

Duplicate Services: Look for categories where you might be paying for similar services from multiple vendors. Common areas include software subscriptions, professional services, and marketing channels.

Underutilized Resources: Identify expenses for resources you're not fully utilizing such as unused software licenses, excessive inventory, or overcapacity service plans.

Efficiency Opportunities: Find categories where spending has grown without corresponding business growth, indicating potential efficiency improvements.

Negotiation Targets: Focus on your largest expense categories for negotiation opportunities. Even small percentage reductions can create significant savings.

Waste Elimination Strategies

Subscription Audits: Review all recurring subscriptions quarterly, canceling unused services and downsizing over-provisioned accounts.

Process Optimization: Identify spending patterns that indicate inefficient processes—excessive rush shipping, duplicate work, or poor planning.

Quality vs. Cost Analysis: Evaluate whether premium-priced vendors are providing proportional value, or if comparable alternatives exist.

Timing Optimization: Look for patterns where better timing could reduce costs. Examples would be bulk purchasing, seasonal negotiations, or strategic vendor management.

Aligning Spending with Strategic Goals

Goal-Based Spending Analysis

Revenue Growth Goals: Ensure marketing and sales expenses align with growth targets. Are you investing enough in customer acquisition? Are you spending in the right channels?

Profitability Goals: Identify expense categories that should scale with revenue versus those that should remain fixed or decrease as a percentage of revenue.

Operational Excellence Goals: Evaluate whether spending on systems, training, and process improvement aligns with efficiency objectives.

Market Position Goals: Assess whether spending on quality, innovation, and customer service supports your desired market positioning.

Strategic Investment Identification

Growth Investments: Identify areas where increased spending could drive revenue growth such as better marketing, improved systems, or expanded capacity.

Efficiency Investments: Find opportunities where upfront spending could reduce ongoing operational costs such as automation software, better equipment, or process improvements.

Risk Mitigation Investments: Evaluate whether current spending adequately addresses business risks including insurance, backup systems, or vendor diversification.

Advanced Pattern Analysis Techniques

Ratio Analysis

Expense-to-Revenue Ratios: Track key ratios like marketing expense to revenue, administrative expense to revenue, and cost of goods sold to revenue.

Efficiency Ratios: Calculate metrics like revenue per employee, expenses per customer, and cost per unit produced.

Growth Ratios: Compare expense growth rates to revenue growth rates to ensure spending discipline during expansion.

Seasonal and Cyclical Analysis

Seasonal Spending Patterns: Understand how your spending needs change throughout the year and plan cash flow accordingly. Using the P.O.T.S.™ method helps you prepare for these seasonal shifts by consistently allocating money to payroll, operating expenses, taxes, and savings—so even during slow seasons, your most important financial obligations are already funded.

Business Cycle Analysis: Identify how spending patterns change during different phases of your business cycle: startup, growth, maturity, or contraction.

Market Cycle Responsiveness: Evaluate how quickly you can adjust spending in response to market changes or economic conditions.

Competitive Benchmarking

Industry Standards: Compare your spending patterns to industry benchmarks to identify areas where you might be over or under-investing.

Best Practice Analysis: Research how successful companies in your industry allocate their spending and identify gaps in your approach.

Performance Correlation: Analyze which spending categories correlate most strongly with business performance and success metrics.

Making Data-Driven Decisions

Monthly Spending Reviews

Establish a monthly routine for analyzing spending patterns:

Variance Analysis: Compare actual spending to budgeted amounts and investigate significant variances.

Trend Identification: Look for spending trends that might indicate emerging opportunities or problems.

Action Item Generation: Convert insights into specific action items for cost optimization or strategic investment.

Quarterly Strategic Reviews

Strategic Alignment Assessment: Evaluate whether spending patterns support your quarterly business objectives.

ROI Analysis: Calculate return on investment for major spending categories and adjust allocations accordingly.

Forecasting Updates: Use spending pattern insights to improve future financial forecasting and budgeting.

Annual Planning Integration

Budget Development: Use historical spending patterns to create more accurate and strategic budgets for the coming year.

Strategic Planning: Incorporate spending pattern insights into annual strategic planning and goal setting.

Resource Allocation: Make informed decisions about resource allocation based on proven spending effectiveness.

The Continuous Improvement Mindset

Analyzing spending patterns is an ongoing practice that becomes more valuable over time, not just a one-time exercise. As you build a historical database of spending information, your ability to identify trends, predict needs, and optimize costs improves dramatically.

The businesses that excel at spending pattern analysis develop a culture of financial curiosity. They ask questions like: "Why did we spend more in this category this month?" "What would happen if we reallocated funds from Category A to Category B?" "How can we maintain quality while reducing costs in this area?"

This analytical approach transforms business owners from reactive expense managers into proactive financial strategists, using spending data to drive growth, improve efficiency, and build sustainable competitive advantages.

> **REMEMBER:** *Your spending patterns are a roadmap to business optimization, but the question is whether you'll make use of that map to navigate toward greater profitability and success.*

Activation #4

Reviewing Your Financial Statements

By analyzing financial statements, you can gain valuable insights into your company's financial health and make informed decisions about how to allocate resources, reduce costs, and grow the business.

In this section, we will explore the different types of financial statements, how to read and interpret them, and how to use them to make informed financial decisions.

ACTION #4

How To Review Your Financial Statements

A financial statement is the lifeblood of any business. You rely on these financial statements to know the condition, performance, and ability to efficiently sustain past and future operations of a particular business. But how do you read these three critical reports?

Profit & Loss Statement

The P&L will help you understand the overall performance and the profit or loss of your business over a given period of time. You should review your P&L statement monthly, quarterly, and annually. You can also review a comparison of the same time period year-over-year. When you pull up the P&L, you should review each line item to verify its accuracy. You can also click on the dollar amount on a line item to open up a transaction report that allows you to view each transaction that contributes to the total. If you find any inaccuracies, this is the time to correct and/or adjust them. Go through each line item to make sure everything looks good.

Balance Sheet

Use the Balance Sheet Statement to review the financial condition of a business on a specific day. Just like the Profit and Loss Statement, you want to review each category to ensure that it is correct. For instance, in the first section is your "assets," which are your bank account balances, compare the amount on your financial report to the balance on your financial institution statement as of that date. Likewise, any credit cards or loans you have should reflect the same balance on your financial report as it does on the statement from the financial institution. If you find any inaccuracies, this is the time to correct and/or adjust them.

Cash Flow Statement

Your cash flow statement provides a detailed picture of what happened to your business cash during a specified period, known as the accounting period. It demonstrates your organization's ability to operate in the short and long term, based on how much cash is flowing into and out of the business. There are two types of Cash Flow Statements: a direct method and an indirect method.

- Direct method presents you with a condensed cash receipts and cash disbursements statement.
- Indirect method presents you with cash movements by adjusting net income for items that affected reported net income but didn't affect cash. For example, it adds back non-cash expenses like depreciation and adjusts for changes in working capital such as accounts receivable, accounts payable, or inventory, This method essentially reconciles your profit on paper with the cash that truly flowed in and out of your business.

Reflection

1. Have there been any significant changes in your spending patterns?

2. Are there any seasonal trends?

3. Are there any areas where spending has increased or decreased significantly or unexpectedly?

10

Understanding Your Financial Statements

• Your roadmap to strategic financial decision-making •

The Foundation of Financial Intelligence

Your financial statements are the strategic intelligence reports that reveal the true story of your business performance, financial position, and operational efficiency. Understanding how to read and interpret these statements transforms you from a business owner who operates on gut feelings to one who makes data-driven decisions with confidence. As you review these reports each year, don't forget to update your business plan to reflect your most current realities and goals. A business plan fueled by up-to-date financial insights becomes a living strategy for growth, while one built on stale numbers is nothing more than a dusty document.

Think of your financial statements as the vital signs of your business. Just as medical professionals use different instruments to assess various aspects of health like blood pressure, heart rate, and temperature, business owners need different financial statements to assess various aspects of business health. We've already discussed these three reports, but now we are going to go a little deeper to help you use these reports to understand the insights they can offer you.

The Profit and Loss Statement: Your Performance Report Card

As you have now learned, the P&L shows your business income and expenses over a specified period of time, whether that's a month, quarter, or year. This statement tells the story of your operational performance and reveals whether your business activities are generating profit or creating losses.

The Monthly Reality Check

Reviewing your P&L monthly provides one of the most powerful reality checks in business ownership. It's one thing to "think" you're spending reasonable amounts in various categories, but seeing the actual numbers on paper often provides surprising, and sometimes shocking, revelations.

Common Eye-Opening Discoveries

- That "small" daily coffee expense actually totals $300 each month.
- Marketing efforts are consuming 25% of revenue instead of the budgeted 10%.
- Office supplies have mysteriously doubled without any obvious reason.
- Labor costs are growing faster than revenue, eroding profitability.
- Subscription services have crept up to significant monthly expenses.

Where Strategic Decisions Begin

The P&L is where strategic financial decision-making truly begins. When you can see exactly how much you're spending in each category, you can begin to align your actual spending with your previously stated business goals. This alignment process involves asking critical questions:

- Does our marketing spend align with our growth objectives?
- Are we investing enough in areas that drive revenue?
- Which expense categories are growing faster than our income?
- Where can we optimize spending without compromising quality or service?
- Are we allocating resources to our highest-priority business objectives?

The Course Correction Opportunity

Monthly or quarterly P&L reviews provide invaluable opportunities for course correction before year-end. Instead of discovering spending overruns during annual tax preparation, regular reviews allow you to make adjustments throughout the year.

Mid-Course Adjustments

- Reduce discretionary spending if expenses are outpacing revenue
- Reallocate marketing budget from underperforming to high-performing channels
- Negotiate better vendor terms for high-volume expense categories
- Identify seasonal patterns and plan cash flow accordingly
- Make strategic investments during profitable periods

This proactive approach prevents small problems from becoming major financial challenges and helps you end the year aligned with your strategic objectives rather than scrambling to understand what happened.

The Balance Sheet Is Your Financial Pulse

While your P&L shows performance over time, your Balance Sheet provides a snapshot of your business financial pulse on a particular day. It reveals what your business owns (assets), what it owes (liabilities), and your ownership stake (equity) at that specific moment.

Monthly Health Monitoring

Reviewing your Balance Sheet monthly ensures accuracy and helps you monitor the overall health and stability of your business. This statement reveals critical information that the P&L doesn't show.

Asset Management

- Cash position and liquidity trends
- Accounts receivable aging and collection efficiency
- Inventory levels and turnover rates
- Equipment and asset utilization

Liability Management

- Outstanding vendor obligations and payment timing
- Debt levels and debt-to-equity ratios

- Credit utilization and available credit capacity
- Working capital trends and seasonal patterns

Equity Growth

- Retained earnings accumulation from profitable operations
- Owner investment and withdrawal patterns
- Business value appreciation over time

Red Flags and Warning Signs

Monthly Balance Sheet reviews help identify potential problems before they become critical. Here are things to watch for:

- Declining cash balances that could signal cash flow problems
- Growing accounts receivable that might indicate collection issues
- Increasing debt levels without corresponding asset growth
- Negative working capital trends that could affect operations

The Cash Flow Statement Is Your Spending Tracker and Budget Guide

The Cash Flow Statement tracks how cash moves through your business during a specific period, showing exactly where cash came from and where it went. This statement bridges the gap between your P&L profitability and your actual cash position.

Understanding Cash vs. Profit

One of the most confusing aspects of business finance is why profitable companies can struggle with cash flow. The Cash Flow Statement explains this seeming contradiction by showing the timing differences between earning revenue and collecting cash or incurring expenses and paying bills.

Operating Activities: Cash generated or used by core business operations

- Collections from customers
- Payments to vendors and employees
- Interest and tax payments

Investing Activities: Cash used for or generated from business investments

- Equipment purchases
- Asset sales
- Business acquisitions or disposals

Financing Activities: Cash from or used for financing the business

- Loan proceeds or payments
- Owner contributions or withdrawals
- Credit line usage

Strategic Cash Flow Management

Regular Cash Flow Statement analysis enables better budgeting and strategic planning.

Predictive Budgeting

- Identify seasonal cash flow patterns for better planning
- Understand the timing between sales and cash collection
- Plan major purchases during cash-positive periods
- Anticipate financing needs during growth phases

Operational Optimization

- Improve accounts receivable collection processes
- Negotiate better payment terms with vendors
- Optimize inventory levels to free up cash
- Time major expenses to align with cash availability

Cash Flow Forecasting

Use historical Cash Flow Statement data to create forward-looking cash flow projections:

- Predict when cash shortfalls might occur
- Plan for seasonal working capital needs

- Evaluate the cash impact of growth opportunities
- Assess the feasibility of major business investments

The Integrated View Is Using All Three Together

The real power comes from using all three statements together to get a complete picture of your business:

Monthly Review Process:

1. Start with the P&L to understand operational performance
2. Review the Balance Sheet to assess financial position
3. Analyze the Cash Flow Statement to understand cash management
4. Look for connections and relationships between the three statements

Strategic Questions to Ask

- Why does our P&L show profit but our cash position is declining?
- How do changes in our Balance Sheet accounts affect cash flow?
- What operational decisions would improve all three statements?
- Where do we see opportunities for optimization across all metrics?

Building Financial Statement Literacy

While your financial statements are, indeed, about compliance and satisfying your accountant, they also are about you building the financial literacy necessary to make informed business decisions. When you can confidently read and interpret these statements, you gain the insights necessary to:

- Negotiate from a position of strength with lenders and investors.
- Make strategic decisions based on facts rather than assumptions.
- Identify opportunities and problems before they become critical.
- Communicate effectively with financial professionals and business partners.
- Plan for growth and expansion with realistic financial projections.

Your financial statements are the vital signs of your business. Learning to read them accurately and consistently is one of the most valuable skills you can develop as a business owner. The monthly discipline of reviewing and understanding these statements transforms you from someone who owns a business to a true CEO who strategically manages a profitable enterprise.

Pro Tip: Take a peek at our complimentary step-by-step tutorial videos to walk you through bookkeeping basics from setting up your software to reading your first financial report. Grab instant access at ***www.triedandtruefs.com/videotutorials***.

11

Making Data-Driven Business Decisions

• Transforming financial insights into strategic action •

From Gut Feelings to Strategic Intelligence

The difference between successful businesses and those that struggle often comes down to one critical factor: the quality of their decision-making. While entrepreneurial intuition has its place, sustainable business success requires decisions based on accurate financial data rather than assumptions or gut feelings.

As we have pointed out several times now, when you consistently maintain accurate books and understand your financial statements, you create a powerful foundation for data-driven decision-making. Your properly categorized transactions, reconciled accounts, and current financial reports become the strategic intelligence that can and should guide every important business choice.

The Power of Financial Data in Decision-Making

Data-driven decisions remove guesswork from business management and replace it with confidence backed by facts. Instead of wondering whether you can afford that new piece of equipment, you know exactly what your cash flow can support. Rather than guessing which marketing channels provide the best return, you can analyze actual spending and revenue data to optimize your marketing allocation.

Key Areas Where Data Drives Better Decisions

Pricing Strategy

Your financial data reveals true costs, including hidden expenses that many business owners overlook. When you understand your complete cost structure, you can price products and services to ensure profitability rather than hoping you're charging enough.

Cash Flow Management

Historical cash flow patterns help you predict future needs, plan for seasonal fluctuations, and avoid cash crunches. You can time major purchases, plan inventory orders, and schedule vendor payments based on proven patterns rather than wishful thinking.

Investment Opportunities

Whether you're considering new equipment, additional staff, or business expansion, your financial data provides the foundation for calculating return on investment and assessing feasibility.

Cost Optimization

Regular analysis of spending patterns reveals opportunities to reduce costs without compromising quality. You might discover you're paying for duplicate services, over provisioned subscriptions, or inefficient processes.

Revenue Enhancement

By analyzing which products, services, or customer segments generate the highest profitability, you can focus your efforts on the most lucrative opportunities.

Turning Reports into Actionable Insights

The key to effective data-driven decision-making lies in knowing which questions to ask of your financial data and how to interpret the answers.

Monthly Decision-Making Questions

Profitability Analysis

- Which products or services generate the highest profit margins?
- Are there expense categories growing faster than revenue?
- Where can we improve efficiency without reducing quality?

Cash Flow Optimization

- What seasonal patterns affect our cash flow?
- Which customers consistently pay late, affecting our cash position?
- How can we better time our payables to optimize cash flow?

Growth Opportunities

- What would be the financial impact of expanding into a new market?
- Can we afford to hire additional staff based on current trends?
- Which marketing channels provide the best return on investment?

Creating Decision-Making Frameworks

Develop systematic approaches to major business decisions

Investment Evaluation Framework

- Analyze current financial position and cash availability
- Project the investment's impact on monthly cash flow
- Calculate break-even timeline and return on investment
- Assess risk factors and contingency plans

Expense Evaluation Process

- Categorize expenses as essential, beneficial, or discretionary
- Analyze spending trends to identify patterns
- Compare costs to industry benchmarks when available
- Evaluate alternatives and negotiate better terms

The Competitive Advantage of Data-Driven Decisions

Businesses that consistently make data-driven decisions gain significant competitive advantages.

Faster Response to Market Changes: When you monitor financial metrics regularly, you can quickly identify trends and adjust strategies before competitors notice the shifts.

Improved Resource Allocation: Data helps you invest time, money, and energy in activities that generate the highest returns, while competitors waste resources on unproductive efforts.

Better Risk Management: Financial data helps you identify potential problems early and take corrective action before they become critical issues.

Enhanced Credibility: When you can support decisions with solid financial data, you build credibility with lenders, investors, partners, and employees.

Building a Data-Driven Culture

Making data-driven decisions becomes easier and more natural when you:

Establish Regular Review Cycles: Schedule monthly sessions to analyze financial data and identify decision-making opportunities.

Create Simple Dashboards: Develop one-page summaries of key financial metrics that you can review quickly and regularly.

Document Decision Rationale: Keep records of why you made specific decisions and track the outcomes to improve future decision-making.

Seek Multiple Perspectives: Use your financial data as a starting point for discussions with advisors, mentors, or business partners.

The Long-Term Impact

Data-driven decision-making creates a virtual cycle: better decisions lead to improved financial performance that, in turn, generate better data for future decisions. Over time, this approach builds a more resilient, profitable, and strategic business that can weather challenges and capitalize on opportunities.

Your investment in maintaining accurate financial records pays its biggest dividends when these records are used to enable confident, strategic decision-making that drives sustainable business growth and success.

Reflection

1. What did you learn about your business accounting this quarter?

2. What are you most proud of?

3. How can you improve next quarter?

12

Preparing for Tax Season

• Setting yourself up for success year-round •

The Foundation of Tax Readiness

Tax season doesn't have to be a stressful scramble through boxes of receipts and frantic attempts to reconstruct financial records. When you maintain a well-organized bookkeeping system throughout the year, tax preparation becomes a smooth, efficient process that actually provides valuable insights into your business performance.

The secret lies in strategic preparation that begins on January 1. By aligning your bookkeeping system with tax requirements from the very start, you create a seamless bridge between daily financial management and annual tax compliance.

The Chart of Accounts Strategy: Your Tax Preparation Secret Weapon

As we pointed out in chapter 3, one of the most powerful strategies for tax season success is structuring your Chart of Accounts to mirror the tax form your business will file. This alignment creates a direct pathway from your daily bookkeeping to your annual tax return, eliminating the need for extensive reorganization and reclassification during tax preparation. For your convenience, these forms are referenced again here.

Business Structure Alignment

Sole Proprietorship (Schedule C): Structure your expense categories to match Schedule C lines, including specific categories for advertising, car and truck expenses, commissions and fees, contract labor, depletion, depreciation, employee benefit programs, insurance, interest, legal and professional services, office expenses, pension and profit-sharing plans, rent or lease, repairs and maintenance, supplies, taxes and licenses, travel, meals, and utilities.

S Corporation (Form 1120-S): Organize accounts to align with Form 1120-S requirements, including officer compensation, salaries and wages, repairs and maintenance, bad debts, rents, taxes and licenses, interest, charitable contributions, depreciation, depletion, advertising, pension and profit-sharing plans, employee benefit programs, and other deductions.

Partnership (Form 1065): Structure categories to match partnership reporting requirements, including salaries and wages, guaranteed payments to partners, interest, taxes and licenses, repairs and maintenance, bad debts, rents, depreciation, depletion, and other specific partnership deductions.

C Corporation (Form 1120): Align accounts with corporate tax reporting categories, including compensation of officers, salaries and wages, repairs and maintenance, bad debts, rents, taxes and licenses, interest, charitable contributions, depreciation, depletion, advertising, and other allowable corporate deductions.

The Accountant's Perspective

Your accountant will absolutely love this strategic approach because it dramatically reduces the time and effort required for tax preparation. Instead of spending hours reorganizing and reclassifying your financial data to fit tax reporting requirements, they can focus on tax compliance and deduction accuracy and optimization.

This efficiency translates into several benefits:

- Reduced preparation fees due to less time spent on data organization
- Faster turnaround times for tax return completion
- More accurate returns due to properly categorized data

Year-Round Tax Planning: Beyond Compliance

While proper bookkeeping sets the foundation for tax success, proactive tax planning throughout the year ensures you're not surprised by your tax liability when filing time arrives. Regular communication with your tax professional enables strategic moves that can significantly impact your tax burden. The cost you will spend on year-round tax planning should be well worth the tax savings you will gain.

Quarterly Tax Planning Sessions

Schedule quarterly meetings with your accountant to review financial performance and implement tax planning strategies:

First Quarter Review (April): Analyze the previous year's tax return results, plan current year estimated tax payments, and discuss any business structure changes that might benefit tax planning.

Second Quarter Review (July): Evaluate mid-year financial performance, assess whether current year projections align with tax planning assumptions, and make adjustments to estimated tax payments if necessary.

Third Quarter Review (October): Analyze year-to-date performance, implement any necessary end-of-year tax planning strategies and finalize equipment purchases or other deductible expenses.

Fourth Quarter Review (January): Conduct final tax planning for the completed year, ensure all deductible expenses are properly recorded, and begin planning for the upcoming tax year.

Strategic Tax Planning Opportunities

Expense Timing: Understanding when to accelerate or defer deductible expenses can significantly impact your tax liability. Your organized bookkeeping system makes it easy to identify opportunities and track the financial impact of timing decisions.

Equipment Purchases: Section 179 deductions and bonus depreciation rules provide opportunities to deduct equipment purchases immediately rather than depreciating them over time. Your financial data helps determine optimal timing for these investments.

Retirement Contributions: Business retirement plan contributions can provide significant tax benefits while helping you save for the future. Regular financial analysis helps determine optimal contribution levels.

Business Structure Optimization: As your business grows and evolves, your current business structure might not be the most tax efficient. Regular financial analysis with your accountant can identify opportunities for beneficial structure changes.

Documentation and Record-Keeping Excellence

Proper documentation throughout the year supports tax compliance and maximizes deductible expenses.

Receipt Management: Implement systems for capturing and storing receipts digitally, ensuring all business expenses are properly documented.

Mileage Tracking: Maintain detailed logs of business travel, including dates, destinations, purposes, and odometer readings.

Home Office Documentation: Keep records supporting home office deductions, including photographs, measurements, and expense allocations.

Business Meal Records: Document business meals with details about attendees, business purposes, and expense amounts.

The Surprise Prevention Plan

Nobody likes tax surprises, especially unexpected large tax bills. Year-round financial management combined with regular tax planning prevents these unpleasant surprises.

Cash Flow Planning for Tax Obligations

Estimated Tax Payments: Use your organized financial data to calculate accurate estimated tax payments, avoiding both underpayment penalties and excessive overpayments.

Tax Reserve Accounts: Establish separate savings accounts for tax obligations, automatically transferring a percentage of revenue to build tax reserves throughout the year.

Year-End Projections: Regularly project year-end tax liability based on current financial performance, allowing time for planning moves to optimize tax outcomes.

Compliance Monitoring

Payroll Tax Compliance: Ensure timely payment of payroll taxes and proper reporting to avoid penalties and interest charges.

Sales Tax Management: If applicable, maintain current sales tax records and remittances to avoid compliance issues.

Information Return Filing: Stay current with required information returns like 1099s to avoid penalties and ensure smooth tax preparation.

The Long-Term Benefits

Investing in proper tax preparation extends far beyond compliance. Well-organized financial records and strategic tax planning provide:

Business Intelligence: Tax preparation processes often reveal trends and opportunities that inform future business decisions.

Audit Protection: Organized records and proper documentation provide strong support if questions arise about your tax returns.

Growth Planning: Understanding your tax obligations helps with cash flow planning and growth strategies.

Professional Relationships: Working proactively with tax professionals builds valuable advisory relationships that benefit your business long-term.

REMEMBER: *While you do want to file your taxes correctly, your goal really is to use the tax preparation process as an opportunity to optimize your financial management, reduce your tax burden legally, and build systems that support sustainable business growth. When tax season becomes a strategic business review rather than a compliance scramble, you've achieved true financial management success.*

CONCLUSION

Your Financial Success Journey

• Embracing your role as a financially empowered business owner •

You've Come Full Circle

Congratulations! You've just completed a comprehensive journey through the essential elements of bookkeeping for small business success. From understanding basic accounting terminology to implementing monthly routines that keep your financial house in order, you now possess the knowledge and tools necessary to take control of your business finances with confidence.

This journey we've taken together represents more than just learning bookkeeping techniques; it's about fundamental transformation. You've evolved from someone who might have felt overwhelmed by financial management to someone equipped with the knowledge, systems, and confidence to make your numbers work for you rather than against you!

The Foundation You've Built

Throughout these chapters, you've constructed a solid financial foundation that will serve your business for years to come.

- You understand the language of business finance, knowing that accounting is simply tracking the flow of money in and out of your company: when, where, what for, and how much.
- You've learned to allocate income into strategic P.O.T.S.™, Payroll, Operating expenses, Taxes, and Savings, to reduce the overwhelm that comes with managing your finances.
- You've learned to set up systems strategically, from creating a chart of accounts that aligns with your tax forms to connecting financial accounts in ways that maximize efficiency while maintaining accuracy.
- You've mastered the art of transaction management, understanding how to categorize like a pro, train your accounting system's AI, and create automation rules that save time while improving accuracy.
- You've discovered the power of financial analysis, learning to read spending patterns, identify optimization opportunities, and align your financial reality with your business goals.
- You've embraced the discipline of monthly routines, understanding that consistent FinancialCPR™ (Categorize, Post, and Reconcile) keeps your business financially healthy and provides the data necessary for strategic decision-making.
- You've learned to interpret your financial statements as strategic intelligence reports that guide everything from daily operational decisions to long-term growth planning.

- You've developed the mindset of data-driven decision-making, moving beyond gut feelings to choices backed by solid financial evidence.

- You've prepared for tax season success, understanding how proper bookkeeping throughout the year creates seamless tax compliance and enables strategic tax planning.

The Ongoing Journey

Each month that you practice the principles in this book, you'll become more proficient, more strategic, and more confident in your financial decision making abilities.

> **REMEMBER:** *Financial mastery isn't a destination, it's an ongoing journey of continuous improvement and growing confidence.*

Your bookkeeping system will continue to evolve with your business. As you grow, you'll add new accounts, refine your categorization strategies, and develop more sophisticated analysis techniques. The foundation you've built here will support this growth and adaptation.

The Ripple Effects of Financial Empowerment

The benefits of mastering your business finances extend far beyond clean books and accurate reports. When you're in control of your financial data, here's what you can accomplish:

- Make faster, more confident business decisions

- Build stronger relationships with lenders, investors, and business partners

- Reduce stress and anxiety about your business financial health

- Create more time for strategic work rather than administrative catch-up

- Position your business for sustainable growth and long-term success
- Develop the financial literacy that enhances every aspect of business ownership

A Message of Encouragement

If you've felt overwhelmed by business finances in the past, know that you were not alone. Every successful business owner has faced the challenge of mastering financial management. The difference between those who thrive and those who struggle isn't natural talent, it's the willingness to learn, implement systems, and maintain consistency.

You now have everything you need to succeed. The knowledge is in your hands, the tools are available, and the systems are waiting to be implemented. The only remaining ingredient is your commitment to consistent action.

Start small if you need to. Implement one chapter's concepts at a time. Build your confidence gradually. Remember that every correctly categorized transaction, every completed reconciliation, and every financial report you review makes you more proficient and more confident.

APPENDICES

APPENDIX 1

Financial Affirmations

As you continue this journey, embrace these affirmations that reinforce your growing financial empowerment and success:

» I am financially abundant.

» I am financially responsible.

» I am knowledgeable about financial principles.

» I am financially free.

» I am financially literate.

» I am in charge of my financial destination.

» I am wealthy.

» I make data-driven decisions that grow my business.

- I understand my numbers and use them strategically.
- I am confident in my financial management abilities.
- My organized financial records support my business success.
- I invest time in financial management because it pays dividends.
- I am building a financially sustainable business.
- My financial discipline creates opportunities for growth.
- I attract abundance through smart financial management.

Repeat these affirmations regularly, especially when facing financial challenges or decisions. They will reinforce the mindset necessary for long-term financial success and help maintain the confidence needed to make strategic financial decisions.

APPENDIX 2

The Path Forward

Your financial success journey doesn't end with this book, it's just beginning! You now have the roadmap, the tools, and the knowledge to build the financially successful business you've always envisioned.

Remember that small businesses are indeed the heartbeat of the American economy, accounting for 99% of all businesses. By mastering your financial management, you're not just improving your own business prospects, you're contributing to the strength and vitality of the entire economic ecosystem.

Your success matters. Your business matters. And now, with the financial knowledge and systems to support your dreams, you're equipped to build the sustainable, profitable business that will provide the freedom, security, and impact you desire.

You've got this! Your books are about to be balanced, your decisions are about to be data-driven, and your business is about to reach new levels of financial success.

The journey continues, and your financial future is bright. To keep your momentum going, I've created a few free resources to help you put what you've learned into action:

The Tried and True Resource Guide

Stay current with the best bookkeeping and accounting software for small businesses. This living guide is updated regularly, so you'll always know what tools are out there and which ones I recommend.

Pro Tip: Download it free at ***www.triedandtruefs.com/resourceguide***

The Tried and True Financial Toolkit

Sometimes it's not about learning more, it's about having the right tools at your fingertips. Inside this toolkit you'll find checklists, templates, and simple guides to help you stay consistent and organized.

Pro Tip: Grab your free toolkit at ***www.triedandtruefs.com/financialtoolkit***

The Tried and True Quick Video Tutorials

If you're anything like me, you need to see things to connect the dots. These less-than-10 minute videos walk you through setting up your software, performing your FinancialCPR™ (Categorize, Post, and Reconcile), and reading your financial statements with ease. Perfect for visual learners without the overwhelm.

Pro Tip: Watch them free at ***www.triedandtruefs.com/videotutorials***

REMEMBER: *This book is your foundation, but your financial journey is ongoing. Use these resources to keep building systems that protect your business, free up your time, and give you confidence in every decision you make.*

I can't wait to see what you create when you step into your role not just as a visionary, but as a legacy builder.

Here's to your continued success and the financially empowered business owner you've become!

ACKNOWLEDGMENTS

First and foremost, I want to thank God for His endless blessings and for placing within me the gift and talent to help others in an area that can feel overwhelming and frustrating. Without Him, none of this would be possible.

To my favorite—and only—daughter, thank you for always supporting me in everything I do. You are my mini-me, my joy, and one of my greatest accomplishments. I am so proud of the incredible woman you've become.

To my late mother, who pushed me hard to be my very best, thank you. Your words of encouragement, and especially hearing you say how proud you were of me before your passing, remain one of my greatest treasures.

To my late sister, who cheered for me throughout my career and the launch of Tried and True Financial Services—thank you for always being in my corner.

To everyone who has supported my vision in any way—through mentorship, consulting, free advice, an encouraging word, a referral, a connection, or a gem of wisdom that moved me forward—I am deeply grateful.

To my incredible editorial review team, your contribution to this book was priceless. You sparked a flame in me I didn't even know was there.

To every client who trusted me with your financial information, thank you for believing in me and allowing me to serve you with care and integrity.

And finally, to you, the reader. Whether you purchased or picked up this book to learn and grow, thank you. I appreciate you more than words can say.

With love and gratitude,

Valaise

ABOUT THE AUTHOR

2025 Detroit City Headshots

Valaise Smith brings nearly 30 years of financial services experience to her work as a trusted tax strategist, advisor, and educator. Throughout her career, she has guided individuals, families, and small business owners through the complexities of financial management, tax compliance, and long-term planning. As the founder of Tried and True Financial Services, she leads with a high-touch Advisory and Compliance approach—helping entrepreneurs make informed decisions, remain audit-ready, and build financially sound businesses.

Her signature ABC's of Finance Framework—Advisory, Bookkeeping, and Compliance—reflect her belief that accurate books are only the beginning. When paired with strategic guidance and regulatory insight, bookkeeping becomes a powerful foundation for clarity, confidence, and sustainable growth.

Valaise's commitment to this work deepened during her own battle with breast cancer. The financial systems she established became a pillar of stability during one of the toughest seasons of her life. Today, she uses that experience to empower business owners to build resilient businesses capable of weathering life's unpredictable challenges.

Known for her relatable teaching style, practical wisdom, and heart for serving God's people, Valaise blends expertise with encouragement. When she's not advising clients or creating financial education tools, she enjoys spending time with family, traveling, riding her motorcycle, and serving in ministry.

Made in the USA
Monee, IL
22 September 2026

63923316R00085